E220 CHURCH

VISION CRECE

APOSTOL MOISES RAMIREZ

2

VISION

CRECE

All biblical scriptures except were noted were taken from King James Version.

Translation: Gerardo Grado
Edited: Moises E. Ramirez
Revised by: Serena Ramirez
Design: Moises E. Ramirez

ISBN: 978-1539874058

Category: Religion / Christian Ministry / Discipleship

Printed by CreateSpace, An amazon.com Company
Available on Kindle and other online stores.

VISION CRECE

Apostle Moises Ramirez

E220 Church
Ministry of Restoration, Deliverance,
and Spiritual Warfare

1241 Cypress St.
Abilene, TX 79601
Phone: 325.603.6230

TABLE OF CONTENTS 7

OBJECTIVES

The objective of Vision Crece is to reach and restore the greatest number of people in the whole world who find themselves lost and captive. May those that read and understand Vision Crece put it into practice in their churches, ministries, cell groups, homes, cities, states, and nations.

Vision Crece is designed to gather the greatest and final harvest in these end times.

Vision Crece deals with how to retain the greatest number of these souls possible.

John 4:35 **"SAY NOT YE, THERE ARE YET FOUR MONTHS, AND THEN COMETH HARVEST? BEHOLD, I SAY UNTO YOU, LIFT UP YOUR EYES, AND LOOK ON THE FIELDS; FOR THEY ARE WHITE ALREADY TO HARVEST."**

INTRODUCTION

Welcome to Vision Crece. In this book you will learn all things related to this vision.

Here we will explain how to rescue the lost and also how to retain those souls that accept Jesus as their savior.

All will learn the tools and strategies that God has given to this ministry through the apostle of the house in order to implement Vision Crece.

It's nothing out of this world. It is what God has already left in his written Word only with new revelation.

I encourage you to enter the world of Vision Crece and become equipped to gather the final harvest of this end time without losing any of them.

PRAYER

Lord Jesus Christ, I ask you to give me understanding, wisdom, and revelation to understand Vision Crece. Awaken in me an insatiable hunger and a compassion for the souls that are lost and captive, so that I can help the brokenhearted and give freedom to the captives. In the Name of Jesus Christ, I ask. Amen.

ABOUT THE AUTHOR

Apostle Moises Ramirez is a man called to expand the kingdom of God here on earth through the supernatural power of God.

Being a Christian most of his life, he founded E220 Ministries in different cities in Texas and in Mexico.

Committed to the Great Commission that Jesus left us before He was ascended to heaven, to *"GO INTO ALL THE WORLD AND MAKE DISCIPLES;"* raising in each of the ministries, disciples who can also transmit the vision.

Within his calling he has the mission to restore and liberate those who are captive through spiritual warfare by evangelizing, discipling, consolidating, and sending each one to go and do the same.

He enrolled to study at CBS in Houston, TX: the area with the most Hispanic population as well as a diversity of study and class opportunities.

He is the author of the book "Manual Of Deliverance" which has been translated to the English language.

He has a Kingdom message which is Christ-centered.

Apostle Moises Ramirez resides in Abilene, TX along with his wife Eva, his son Moises Eiroito, and his daughter-in-law Serena. Together they have raised what is today the ministry of restoration, spiritual warfare, and deliverance.

ACKNOWLEDGMENTS

I thank God for my beloved wife, my son, and now also my daughter-in-law who have been by my side in the most difficult moments of my life; for knowing how to comfort me when I most need it and for respecting and honoring my paternity.

A "thank you" for all of the leaders and disciples in the different ministries of E220 and all the members in general who have believed in me and my calling.

Thanks to Gerardo "Jerry" Grado for translating this book to English so that more people may be blessed.

To all of them, I give my greatest and most sincere gratitude, I love all of them in the Lord and they are a part of my life.

Blessings
Moises Ramirez

PART ONE

CHAPTER I

WHAT IS VISION CRECE?

It's an operation that was birthed from the heart of God to gather the final harvest of these last days. It's a tool given by God for the retentions of these souls in the church of Christ once they have accepted Jesus Christ as their savior.

Vision Crece was birthed approximately eight years ago when a book called Operation 72 by Apostle Marcelino Sojo came into my hands. At this time we were pastoring the youth group where we were congregating.

It seemed so interesting to me, especially the area regarding "consolidation".

When Vision Crece came to me the idea of the vision was clear though God had yet to reveal the name.

As time passed, God continued to reveal to me with more clarity what is today Vision Crece.

Vision Crece was not born overnight; it's a work of approximately eight years where God has been in charge of increasing revelation regarding this vision.

Vision Crece was born due to the great need that God has placed in my heart regarding the souls that are losing themselves and are captive; and there are very few who will set them free.

Vision Crece is based on the scripture:

Luke 4:18 *"THE SPIRIT OF THE LORD IS UPON ME, BECAUSE HE HATH ANOINTED ME TO PREACH THE GOSPEL TO THE POOR; HE HATH SENT ME TO HEAL THE BROKENHEARTED, TO PREACH DELIVERANCE TO THE CAPTIVES, AND RECOVERING OF SIGHT TO THE BLIND, TO SET AT LIBERTY THEM THAT ARE BRUISED,"*

This scripture is the heart of Vision Crece, since this is what Jesus came to do while He was on the Earth.

There is a great need in the souls that are suffering with broken hearts, roots of bitterness, pain, lack of forgiveness, rejection, depression, etc. etc. and there is no-one to help them.

I am speaking of those in the churches; Christians, whom while praising, preaching, speaking in tongues, and whatever else they may do, are captive in one area of their life or another.

Christians in church are trapped in addictions, drugs, adultery, pornography, and many other types of sins. They want to escape all this, but are unable and unfortunately in their churches there is no one who can help them. Vision Crece, through the ministry of deliverance, takes the charge to deliver and restore these souls.

Vision Crece is designed so that the souls that accept Christ as savior will not leave the church in the future; it also has the goal of restoring these souls in every aspect of their lives. So, this is what Vision Crece is in a nutshell.

As you read this book, surely you will understand it more with each passing day.

I recommend you pray to God before you implement this vision in your congregation. If God has already confirmed it to you, I then recommend you read this book however many times necessary before applying Vision Crece.

If you have any questions, don't hesitate to contact us by phone, to the number that is published in this book. We are here to serve you without asking you for a commitment.

Blessings.

CHAPTER II

STARTING OVER

The planet on which we live is ruled by laws: laws that are written and placed by God. Even if we may not know them, they are always in motion. For example, the law of gravity, the law of aerodynamics, the law of sowing and reaping, and many other laws that God has placed so this planet could be ruled by them.

"Starting Over" is also based on a law called ground zero. The law of ground zero is to begin again. Everyone at one time or another applies the law of ground zero. The fact that you did not know about it, does not mean you haven't applied it. You apply this law at different stages of your life.

When you begin preschool, elementary school, high school, a new job, any new project in your life, etc.., you're applying the law of ground zero, or: starting over. (When you change cities, move into a new home; begin a new life in Christ, etc.)

Even within the things of God we must start over many times. We need to analyze our lives and stop doing what is bad and begin again.

We regularly apply this law every New Year. We decide and propose to ourselves the new goals that we want to obtain that year.

In order to apply VISION CRECE we need to apply the law of ground zero: STARTING OVER.

Let's look into a Bible story where the law of ground zero was applied.

Genesis 13:3-9 *"AND HE WENT ON HIS JOURNEYS FROM THE SOUTH EVEN TO BETHEL, UNTO THE PLACE WHERE HIS TENT HAD BEEN AT THE BEGINNING, BETWEEN BETHEL AND HAI; UNTO THE PLACE OF THE ALTAR, WHICH HE HAD MAKE THERE AT THE FIRST: AND THERE ABRAM CALLED THE NAME OF THE LORD. AND LOT ALSO, WHICH WENT WITH ABRAM, HAD FLOCKS, AND HERDS, AND TENTS. AND THE LAND WAS NOT ABLE TO BEAR THEM, THAT THEY MIGHT DWELL TOGETHER: FOR THEIR SUBSTANCE WAS GREAT, SO THAT THEY COULD NOT DWELL TOGETHER. AND THERE WAS STRIFE BETWEEN THE HERDSMEN OF ABRAM'S CATTLE AND THE HERDSMEN OF LOT'S CATTLE: AND THE CANAANITE AND THE PERIZZITE DWELLED THEN IN THE LAND. AND ABRAM SAID UNTO LOT, LET THERE BE NO STRIFE, I PRAY THEE, BETWEEN MY HERDSMEN AND THY HERDSMEN; FOR WE BE BRETHREN. IS NOT THE WHOLE LAND BEFORE THEE? SEPARATE THYSELF, I PRAY THEE,*

FROM ME: IF THOU WILT TAKE THE LEFT HAND, THEN I WILL GO TO THE RIGHT; OR IF THOU DEPART TO THE RIGHT HAND, THEN I WILL GO TO THE LEFT."

Let's study this passage carefully, Abram applied the law of "Starting Over" in this stage of his life.

The third verse says that Abram had returned to his sojourning, the Bible says that he returned to the place his tent was at in the beginning. By this we understand that Abram's life was monotonous and full of routine. In a routine filled life nothing different takes place, nothing new occurs. Whoever has this type of life is afraid of change.

Do you know a church like this? Everything is a routine? Nothing new happens? It's always the same thing: grandma's songs, every year it is the same program, the same preaching, you know who is taking an offering; you know who is next on the program. Nothing happens spontaneously. There are no new souls. There are no miracles. Demons are not cast out. It's always the same old, same old.

Abram found himself as many Christians nowadays, going in circles from the church to the house, from the house to the job, and this gets repeated every day as a routine. He lived going in circles from the Negev to Bethel and from Bethel to Hai. This was Abram's life, full of routine without new experiences.

When God has a purpose in you, and your life is in the same state as Abram's was, God has to do something so that His purpose will be fulfilled. Let's see what God did in this story in order to fulfill the purpose in Abram's life.

God allows for there to be a family conflict between Abram and his nephew, Lot. Many times family conflicts that happen to you in life are not to destroy you. Rather, they serve to help you react and leave that routine filled life you are living.

God allowed Abram and his nephew Lot to have a fight due to the cattle and in that way to separate the two. Remember the mandate for Abram was for him to leave his country **and** kindred. Abram had left his country but not all of his kindred. God needed to do something so that His purpose could be fulfilled in Abram. Abram understood that there was a curse on his life and it was necessary to remove that curse. He understood that what was holding him back was his nephew, Lot. He had to make a decision. He told his nephew that it was time to separate.

There are moments in our lives where we need to make decisions, sometimes painfully, but it is so that the purpose of God can be fulfilled. One of the most difficult times in a person's life is when the time comes to make changes. We can see our own suffering, everything we touch falls apart, but we don't want to make changes. You know that your smoking addiction is killing you, but you won't stop. Drinking soft drinks are causing so many diseases, but we won't leave it. We don't like change. We are so used to the routine that it's difficult for us to accept we are wrong.

This is how ordinary Abram's life was, there was no advancement.

ROUTINE WILL HOLD BACK THE PURPOSES OF GOD IN YOUR LIFE

There came a time in the life of Abram that he had to apply the law of "Starting Over."

There are moments in life in which it is necessary to halt and observe what is happening to us; to reflect and to make the decisions necessary to make changes in life. The same thing happens in our ministry, calling, vocation, business, profession, etc. etc. etc.

Let's speak of what has been happening in churches these last few decades. The majority of churches nowadays, with few exceptions, run like Abram's life: full of routine, boring, with little to nothing new happening. These are churches that claim to belong to Christ but nothing manifests, no miracles, no healings, no deliverance, nothing new or different. Everything is programmed, exactly the same always.

The worst thing that is happening to these churches is that if you tell them what is happening in other churches, they have no reaction. They're comfortable. They don't want changes in their church for fear of people leaving. In order to apply Vision Crece it is then necessary to make changes in our lives and in the church in general. We cannot apply Vision Crece with the same old way of thinking.

We need to begin to renew our minds. There is no Vision Crece in an old wine mentality. Vision Crece is new wine. God cannot pour new wine in an old vessel because it will be wasted. To apply Vision Crece we will need to start over. As God was revealing these things to me He told me, "It's necessary to preach again unto my church because we've been doing things the wrong way." He was referring to the retention of souls.

Jesus said in John 17:12, *"....THOSE THAT THOU GAVEST ME I HAVE KEPT, AND NONE OF THEM IS LOST, BUT THE SON OF PERDITION; THAT THE SCRIPTURE MIGHT BE FULFILLED."*

If we can see what Jesus is saying it is this; Jesus took care of the disciples, and due to his good care, none of them were lost. Nowadays this work of caring for the new converts is not being done correctly and the result of this is that many of those that get saved are eventually lost.

Vision Crece deals with the caring of these newborn babies so that they will remain in the congregations. But we cannot apply Vision Crece without making changes in our lives in order to start over.

VISION CRECE is:
1. A new beginning
2. A new awakening
3. A new genesis
4. A new initiation
5. Starting Over

Abram understood that his life was stuck in monotony and he had to make a decision in his life.
BETHEL = HOUSE OF GOD
HAI = RUIN, MISERY, DESOLATION

See how the life of Abram was: at times in the house of God and at times in misery, at times in blessings and in other times in ruins and desolations.

This same thing is happening to many children of God. Since they are unable to secure the blessings of God in their lives sometimes they are in the house of God and then at others they are away from God. They go through this cycle yearly. By the time they've figured it out, they've flunked another year and have to begin with the same routine the next year.

CHANGES

It's time to make changes in our lives and in the church so we can start over. Everything that distracts you, confuses you, takes your money, and everything that traps you has to end today in the Name of Jesus Christ. Everything that brings with it pain, annoyance, sickness, and suffering: all of this has to be cut off. We need to cut off all of the "Lots" of our lives: the relationships that waste your time, the friendships that distract you, the relatives that hinder your life and halt your spiritual growth, the unnecessary phone calls, and the Facebook contacts. Everything! It must all be cut off and dismissed just as Abram did with Lot.

CONCLUSION

I declare that this is the time God has chosen for your life. This is the season you've been waiting for. It's time to start over. It's a time of new beginnings in your life. It's time for a new awakening. A new genesis is waiting for you just up ahead. You have to make decisions, hard as they may be, you must dare to. Life is full of decision making opportunities and those who refuse will be stuck; yet those that make them are people of great success.

Your life today is the result of yesterday's decisions; in other words, what you are now is a product of your past decisions.

There are many souls that are being lost and no one cares to do anything. If this book has interested you, it's because God has placed in you a burden for the souls, but you don't know yet what to do. Good! I encourage you to continue learning Vision Crece and in the end you will be ready to retain those new souls in your congregation.

CHAPTER III

THE FAMILY ALTAR

The family altar is setting aside at least one hour of prayer in the early morning between three to six a.m. where you can worship and praise, but above all where you can intercede for the future harvest of souls that God already has prepared.

PRAYING IN THE MORNING

I will only touch upon one biblical passage regarding the Morning Prayer since we will deal with it in more depth in the next chapter. Without prayer there is no harvest and without prayer there is no consolation. Prayer is part of the daily life of every citizen of the kingdom of God, but to pray in the morning is even more effective.

Mark 1:35 *"AND IN THE MORNING, RISING UP A GREAT WHILE BEFORE DAY, HE WENT OUT, AND DEPARTED INTO A SOLITARY PLACE, AND THERE PRAYED."*

Jesus left us a great example of prayer in the morning. In the morning there is not a lot of distraction.

God speaks in the morning. God hears your morning prayers.

Witches also pray in the early morning hours, and the church is asleep. This is why we are losing the battle. We must pray in the morning in order to undo all of the designs of the devil against you and your family.

Well, we will speak much more about early Morning Prayer in the next chapter.

THE FAMILY ALTAR

The family altar is where the entire family gathers in a place in the home that has been previously chosen to give God a daily sacrifice together as a family: sacrifices of praise and worship and above all, to intercede for souls.

During this family altar you will also pray spiritual warfare prayers against the works of the devil and at the end of your time with God, every day you should end partaking of the Lord's Supper.

In the place you already chose to gather every day, there should be a small table with the elements for the Lord's super; grape juice and bread are the elements to partake of the Lord's super at the family altar. In order to speak about this communion we will look at many passages in the Bible:

Acts 2:42 *"AND THEY CONTINUED STEADFASTLY IN THE APOSTLES' DOCTRINE AND FELLOWSHIP, AND IN BREAKING OF BREAD, AND IN PRAYERS."*

COMMUNION = A union of two or more people who believe the same thing

To be able to carry, out the family altar and partake of the Lord's Supper, you and I must be in one accord. The first believers in the primitive church were all in one accord. Remember that they had JUST been saved and baptized. We should observe with attention what the primitive church did with these newly convert.

1. They persevered in the doctrine of the apostles.
2. They continued in fellowship one with another.
3. In the breaking of bread.
4. Prayer.

These are four things that the primitive church would do. If we would do what they did, we would have the results they had. The people were filled with fear because of the things they did; signs and wonders were a part of their daily life. It was normal for them to do all kinds of miracles. All of this would happen because they were all in one accord. In prayer, they shared in the breaking of bread and in all the apostles would teach them.

If the church of the 21st century would understand these things, the same would happen. But, at the outset, many Christians nowadays don't even believe in apostles, much less in having all things in common one with another.

This is why nothing happens in many churches, because they're all fighting among each other. So if we speak about the Lord's Supper we need to be in one accord; this is communion.

Now in verse 46 of this same chapter tells us they shared in the breaking of bread in homes. The Lord's Supper is also to be celebrated in the homes. In fact, the actual Lord's Supper was celebrated in a home.

I will explain what we believe about the Lord's Supper, I know this explanation will destroy many theologies about it. My purpose is for you to understand what the primitive church practiced.

Nowadays many don't even celebrate the Lord's Supper and those that do, do so because it's a tradition and not because they have a revelation to do so. It's necessary to learn this so you can practice it in your family altar and do it with knowledge.

Genesis 14:18-20 *"AND MELCHIZEDEK KING OF SALEM BROUGHT FORTH BREAD AND WINE: AND HE WAS THE PRIEST OF THE MOST HIGH GOD. AND HE BLESSED HIM, AND SAID, BLESSED BE ABRAM OF THE MOST HIGH GOD, POSSESSOR OF HEAVEN AND EARTH AND BLESSED BE THE MOST HIGH GOD, WHICH HATH DELIVERED THINE ENEMIES INTO THY HAND. AND HE GAVE HIM TITHES OF ALL"*

I will try to explain this passage in the simplest way possible.

FIRST: In these verses we find the first instance in the entire Bible, the Lord's Supper. We know that Melchizedek is a type and a shadow of the Lord Jesus Christ. Then, the man that appeared unto Abram is the Lord Jesus Christ. the man that celebrates this supper with Abram is the Lord. The Bible says in the book of Revelation that God has made us kings and priests. So the first thing we learn in practicing the Lord's Supper is that God is restoring in us the Melchizedechial priesthood.

SECONDLY: *"And he gave him tithes of all."* God gives him the bread and the wine, and Abram gives God the tithes of all. This is a covenant between God and Abram. Then, when you celebrate the Lord's Supper and you are faithful with your tithes, you are making a covenant with God. Giving your tithes is more than giving your money. It's a covenant, if you are also celebrating the Lord's Supper.

NAMES FOR THE LORD'S SUPPER

1. Holy supper
2. Communion
3. Passover
4. The Eucharist

The devil made it his job to distort what the Lord's Supper is for Christians and for the same reason we don't give it its rightful importance. The apostle Paul mentions in 1 Corinthians 10:16 *"THE CUP OF BLESSING WHICH WE BLESS, IS IT NOT THE COMMUNION OF THE BLOOD OF CHRIST? THE BREAD WHICH WE BREAK, IS IT NOT THE COMMUNION OF THE BODY OF CHRIST?"* The Apostle Paul calls it the COMMUNION of the body of Christ.

COMMUNION = KOINONIA = Fellowship, friendship, common union, community, sharing something with someone.

God shared His Son with us and we, in celebrating communion, remember what He did for each one of us. Jesus shared His body and His blood for each one of us.

What unites us is not a religion, denomination, organization, or doctrines of man. No! It's the body of Christ, or at least this is what the Apostle Paul says. This is why we're all divided into denominations, false doctrines, organizations, and other sectors of christianity. Because we have not learned to have KOINONIA with each other; and all because we lack understanding about the communion of the Lord, Many have a half communion with God based on what they believe or what is convenient for them. But once we talk about the Lord's Supper, they would rather not partake.

This is why we have apathetic churches which are spiritually dead because they are not communing with the Lord. When you are in common accord with Him who saved you, you do what He did. You could be doing what Jesus would be doing if He were still on the earth.

ASPECTS OF COMMUNION WITH THE LORD

1 Corinthians 11:26 *"FOR AS OFTEN AS YE EAT THIS BREAD, AND DRINK THIS CUP, YE DO SHEW THE LORD'S DEATH TILL HE COME."*

> FIRST: Shew his death
> SHEW = to proclaim, declare, announce with a loud voice
> WHAT DO YOU SHEW? His death.
> TO WHOM? To humanity and to the demons.

Every time we participate in communion we are preaching with our example to our family, our family in Christ, and those that surround us; when you are constantly participating of the Lords supper, you become bolder, more daring, and more secure in yourself.

SECOND: When you participate in communion with the Lord, you are announcing to the devil and his demons what Jesus did on the cross with each one of them. You remind them that He publicly shamed them on the cross.

ONE MORE THING: 1 Corinthians 11:25 *"... THIS DO YE, AS OFT AS YE DRINK IT, IN REMEMBRANCE OF ME."*

What does **"IN REMEMBRANCE OF ME"** mean?

One of the meanings is as if you were turning back time and going back to the place where these things happened. When Jesus says to do it "in remembrance of me", He is saying to return to the time and place where I was sacrificed for you. Live what I lived. Feel what I felt. Suffer what I suffered. "In remembrance of me" is to live what Jesus lived.

This is why many Christians today are not sensitive to what humanity is living; because we have not suffered what He suffered or felt what he felt.

To be able to apply Vision Crece we need to be sensitive to the pain of souls; their sufferings, feeling what they feel.

"THIS DO YE, AS OFT AS YE DRINK IT"

What are some aspects of the Lord's communion?

1.   To announce His death to the devil, demons, and humanity.
2.   In remembrance of me is to live what Jesus lived
3.   "as oft as ye drink it""

I ask you, how often do you announce His death? Every year or every day? Do you only want to remind the devil of his defeat once a year? Do you only want to remember what Jesus did for you on the cross once a year? I am certain that your answer is no. At least I know I want to do it every day. "As oft as ye drink it." I want to remind the devil every day that he and his demons are defeated. I remind him as the Apostle Paul says, by celebrating communion with the Lord.

In the times of the church we are living the true meaning has been lost. Everything that has been done differently to the way God established must be restored. We know God is restoring all things. Likewise, God is restoring the Lord's communion.

JOHN 6:27-58

If you read this Bible passage the apostle John is speaking about the Lord's Supper. I'll explain without belaboring every detail what the Apostle is saying. They are the words of Jesus that John has written down. Jesus is telling us not to strive for physical food that perishes, rather for the spiritual food set for eternal life. Two types of food are mentioned here: spiritual and physical. Jesus tells us to work for this spiritual food as opposed to the physical one. It continues to explain that the Son of man is the one who gives of this spiritual food, that is to say Jesus does as this was the will of the Father.

Now, remember that Jesus is the one that gives us of the spiritual food. In verse 28 the disciples ask him what they must do to put into practice the work of God.

Note here that the disciples want to do the work of God. The same thing happens with many Christians in these times. They want to do the work of God, but don't in the end. The remainder of the verses in the passage is Jesus's response to their question.

Let's see what Jesus has to tell all of us who want to do His work. In verse 29 Jesus begins His answer to their question. The first thing Jesus teaches them is to believe in Him who sent Him.

Why then does nothing happen in many churches nowadays? It's because we are not believing as we should. We believe in some things of God but in others we don't. Some believe in some things and others believe other things and we are unable to come into agreement. There is no communion.

I hope that you and I can come into agreement regarding the subject of the Lord's communion. Remember that Jesus says we need to believe in Him who sent Him.

In verse 30 the disciples then make two other questions that fit within the first one they had already made. What sign do you produce so we can see and believe? What work do you do? They wanted to know what Jesus was doing. They wanted to know His secret. They were hungry to do the work of God.

In verses 31-34, Jesus continues to answer all of their questions they had just made. We see that Jesus continues to talk first about spiritual food, just like He did with the first question. It seems not to go but Jesus knows the answer and He is going to explain it little by little so they can understand. Jesus begins with the bread that Moses gave in the desert and clarifies that God is the one who gives the true bread from heaven. He tells them that the true bread is that which descends from heaven and that bread is life for the world.

If we understand, Jesus is referring to Himself. The disciples, since they want to do the work of God, they tell Jesus to give them always of this bread.

In verse 35, Jesus tells them He is the bread.

In verse 36, Jesus reminds them of their unbelief.

In verses 41 and 42, the people begin to murmur because Jesus has just said that He was the bread that descended from heaven. They didn't believe that He was the bread and that same thing happens to many Christians today; unbelievers, they do not believe Jesus is the bread. And if He's bread, we must eat it.

In verse 51 Jesus is even more specific and clarifies that He is the bread and whoever eats of this bread will live forever. He also states that the bread He is referring to is His FLESH.

Look well at this verse. It does not say that the bread REPRESENTS OR SYMBOLIZES his flesh. It clearly states that the bread IS HIS FLESH. Remember, Jesus is speaking of food that is spiritual, not physical.

In verse 42 the people believed He was referring to his physical flesh.

In verse 53 Jesus reiterates, if you don't eat of my flesh and drink of my blood, there is no life in you. Those listening couldn't understand. I hope that you, reading this chapter of the book, have come to understand what Jesus is saying.

Now, how are many Christians today? They are lifeless. They are sick physically as well as spiritually. This is because they are not eating and drinking as He told us to.

In verse 54 Jesus repeats that we are to eat His flesh and drink His blood to obtain eternal life. Many want eternal life without eating His flesh and drinking His blood. They have forgotten what is communion with

Christ. They have left the remembrance of what Jesus did for them on the cross and that there He also defeated the devil and his demons. They are not living under the covenant of communion. This is why the condition of many Christians is living from defeat to defeat when the Bible tells us to live from victory to victory.

In verse 55 Jesus is reminding, reiterating, and ratifying that His flesh is true food and his blood is true drink.

In verse 56 Jesus says something very interesting. He says that if we want to remain in Him, we need to eat of His flesh and drink His blood. Why do many not remain in Christ? Because they are not participating in communion with Christ and those that do practice it, do it without understanding. If we want to remain in Christ, we need to participate of His flesh and blood.

In verse 57 Jesus says that He who eats of Jesus will live by Him.

And in verse 58, He ends by telling them again that He is the bread that descended from Heaven. The revelation to all of this is that we must participate of this communion with Christ. In doing so, we understand that the bread is His flesh and the fruit of the vine is his blood. Not that the bread represents his flesh and that the wine represents his blood; rather the bread and wine ARE his flesh and blood respectively. Our bodies receive the bread, but our spirits receive His flesh. The body receives the wine, but our spirits receive His blood.

If we participate of communion then we shall be covered in His blood inside and out every day.

The devil and his demons upon seeing us, will not see us, they will see the blood that is covering us. All of this is what is happening when we practice raising up a family altar. The priest of the home is He who administers communion with His family.

CONCLUSION

If you want to apply the family altar with your family, I hope that this study was of much blessing. But remember, the family altar is a part of Vision Crece.

Blessings.

CHAPTER IV

THE MORNING PRAYER

PRAYER is the time that each believer should pass with his creator to receive instructions and in that way be able to confront the challenges of the day and to intercede for the new harvest.

PRAYER:
- Makes us sensitive to the voice of God.
- Delivers us from pride and arrogance.
- Gives us love for souls.
- Makes us live by faith.
- Submits our flesh and our senses.
- Allows us to see people as God sees them.
- Will not allow us to see the errors in others.
- Will remove all confusion, fear, and insecurities.

Through prayer God gives us instructions.

A life of prayer:
- Will have our spirit controlling our soul
- Will have the spirit controlling the flesh
- Will maintain you firm if someone abandons you
- Will make you successful in all things

A believer without prayer is a lifeless believer. Jesus, before He chose His disciples, prayed all night. He sacrificed. He had been asking the Father what it is He was to do.

Mark 1:35 *"AND IN THE MORNING, RISING UP A GREAT WHILE BEFORE DAY, HE WENT OUT, AND DEPARTED INTO A SOLITARY PLACE, AND THERE PRAYED."*

Jesus, who is our example, prayed early in the morning. This practice must have some secret!

THE TIME

In order to understand this Morning Prayer, it is necessary to understand how to manage time well. If a disciple doesn't manage his time well, time will always escape him and he will never advance in life. If a disciple doesn't know how to manage time well, that disciple will be a hindrance to the work. If a disciple doesn't give the necessary importance to time management, this disciple will invest his time in unimportant things.

Jesus knew the importance of good time management. This is why He would pray early in the morning.

DANGERS OF BAD TIME MANAGEMENT

Bad time management brings along with it:
* Fatigue
* Lethargy
* Frustration
* Bitterness
* Hurt
* Illnesses
* Death

These are the symptoms of a society that lives so hurriedly without learning how to manage time well. When someone accepts Jesus Christ as his or her savior, they bring with them the error of bad time management.

I encourage you to renounce everything that wastes your time. Renounce unnecessary phone calls, TV shows, harmful visits, Facebook, unnecessary trips, and everything that the devil's agenda has for you to waste your time on. What the devil wants is for you to spend hours, days, weeks, months, and years so that in the end, you accomplish nothing. Understand that the devil's agenda is in place for your time to be wasted.

Just as God has an agenda for you, the devil has devised an agenda of distraction for you, I encourage you to reflect and stop wasting time. There are many leaders that are not taking advantage of the time, doing things that God never sent them to do. These things in and of themselves are not bad, but they are still wasting time on things God never mandated. Let's look at a biblical example. Peter understood what time management was.

Acts 6:2 *"THEN THE TWELVE CALLED THE MULTITUDE OF THE DISCIPLES UNTO THEM, AND SAID, IT IS NOT REASON THAT WE SHOULD LEAVE THE WORD OF GOD, AND SERVE TABLES."*

It is not a bad thing to serve tables. To the contrary, Jesus taught us to serve. But, if I do not understand time management, I'll spend my time doing good things and have no time to do what God actually called me to do. Consequently, this is a waste of time.

Peter understood this and reacted by saying: it's not good that the apostles serve tables. I repeat that it wasn't a bad thing to do; it's that their time required more of them. Then the serving at the tables can now be done by others, but the ministry of the Word of God had been given to them.

This same thing is happening today in many churches. Because there is no real time management they fill calendars with so many activities without a clear objective. Just to make noise. But what God wants us to do, we aren't doing. This is time wasted. Jesus tells us to not stop doing one thing while doing the other.

What God truly cares about are the souls that are being lost. God is a God of priorities and if we understand His priorities, we will find out that we are losing time. The Apostle Paul also understood what it is to manage time well.

Ephesians 5:15-17 *"SEE THEN THAT YE WALK CIRCUMSPECTLY, NOT AS FOOLS, BUT AS WISE, REDEEMING THE TIME, BECAUSE THE DAYS ARE EVIL. WHEREFORE BE YE NOT UNWISE, BUT UNDERSTANDING WHAT THE WILL OF THE LORD IS."*

What the Apostle Paul is saying is we must be careful how we are living; be it as wife or fools. He says we need to be wise in order to understand what the will of the Lord is. He continues to say that the wise redeem the time and likewise the foolish waste it.

The will of the Lord then, is to His children to take wise advantage of the time and to tend to the souls is of the wise.

LIFETIME TABLE

Let's suppose that a person dies at 90 years old. Scientists say that daily we have:
* 8 hours to sleep
* 8 hours to work
* 8 hours to rest

If we take this timeline than this person spent his life as follows:
* 30 years sleeping
* 30 years working

- 30 years resting

My question is; is that what God sent us to the earth for? To sleep for 30 years? And resting another 30? No, and again no! I refuse to believe this. God sent us to be productive. We need to be wise and take advantage of time.

Jesus knew these things, that's why He prayed early in the morning.

WHY PRAY IN THE EARLY MORNING?

- In the early morning our minds are clear.
- In the early morning there is no distraction.
- In the early morning you can confront the challenges of the day.
- Jesus healed the sick in the early Morning Prayer.
- Throughout the day He would manifest what He had already accomplished in the early Morning Prayer.
- It's in early Morning Prayer that you win the battles of the day.
- Did you know that witches regularly finish their prayers at about 3am?
- We should come in after 3am and undo the witches' prayers.

AT WHAT TIME IS "IN THE MORNING"?

The people of Israel used to divide the night into three vigils: from 6pm to 10pm, from 10pm to 2am, and from 2am to 6am.

The romans divided the night into four vigils: from 6pm to 9pm, from 9pm, to 12am, from 12 am to 3am and from 3am to 6am.

This is where the bible speaks of the night vigil, the midnight vigil, and the morning vigil. When the bible says the morning vigil it's referring to that vigil that falls from 3am to 6am or before those first sun rays. That's why it says, that Jesus rose early in the morning while it was yet dark.

BENEFITS OF EARLY MORNING PRAYER

Joshua 6:12- *"AND JOSHUA ROSE EARLY IN THE MORNING, AND THE PRIESTS TOOK UP THE ARK OF THE LORD."*

Here the battle began in the morning. The bible tells us that we are in battle. The question is at what time does your daily battle begin?

If Vision Crece is about gathering a harvest of souls, then we are speaking of battle and we need to cover the newborns with prayer in the morning. When you invest time in prayer in the morning, the burdens of the day become lighter.

IF YOU PRAY IN THE MORNING:
- ✓ Your time is better managed.
- ✓ You come into agreement with God's Spirit in everything.
- ✓ You receive revelation of what you have to do that day.

- ✓ God reveals the traps the devil has set for you that day.
- ✓ Falling into temptation is less likely.
- ✓ You protect your disciples that day.
- ✓ You will know what to do that day.

EARLY MORNING PRAYER WILL PRODUCE THE HARVEST

Genesis 1:11-13 *"AND GOD SAID, LET THE EARTH BRING FORTH GRASS, THE HERB YIELDING SEED, AND THE FRUIT TREE YIELDING FRUIT AFTER HIS KIND, WHOSE SEED IS IN ITSELF, UPON THE EARTH: AND IT WAS SO. AND THE EARTH BROUGHT FORTH GRASS, AND HERB YIELDING SEED AFTER HIS KIND, AND THE TREE YIELDING FRUIT, WHOSE SEED WAS IN ITSELF, AFTER HIS KIND: AND GOD SAW THAT IT WAS GOOD. AND THE EVENING AND THE MORNING WERE THE THIRD DAY."*

NOTE: God relates everything that gives fruit to the morning. Trees regularly reproduce in the morning. If we want to gather the harvest of souls, it will have to be done with the early Morning Prayer.

1 Samuel 1:19-20 *"AND THEY ROSE UP IN THE MORNING EARLY, AND WORSHIPPED BEFORE THE LORD, AND RETURNED, AND CAME TO THEIR HOUSE TO RAMAH: AND ELKANAH KNEW HANNAH HIS WIFE; AND THE LORD*

REMEMBERED HER. WHEREFORE IT CAME TO PASS, WHEN THE TIME WAS COME ABOUT AFTER HANNAH HAD CONCEIVED, THAT SHE BARE A SON, AND CALLED HIS NAME SAMUEL, SAYING, BECAUSE I HAVE ASKED HIM OF THE LORD."

Ana was infertile and God remembered her when she and her husband worshiped in the morning. God heard their morning worship. God heard Ana and her husband and gave them a son. They worshipped in the morning and when they had relations later, God gave them the harvest.

YOU CAN FIND GOD IN THE MORNING

Proverbs 8:17 *"I LOVE THEM THAT LOVE ME; AND THOSE WHO SEEK ME EARLY SHALL FIND ME."*

God likes for us to seek Him in the morning.

THE CHILDREN ARE PROTECTED IN THE MORNING PRAYER

Job 1:5 *"AND IT WAS SO, WHEN THE DAYS OF THEIR FEASTING WERE GONE ABOUT, THAT JOB SENT AND SANCTIFIED THEM, AND ROSE UP EARLY IN THE MORNING, AND OFFERED BURNT OFFERINGS ACCORDING TO THE NUMBER OF THEM ALL: FOR JOB SAID, IT MAY*

BE THAT MY SONS HAVE SINNED, AND CURSED GOD IN THEIR HEARTS. THUS DID JOB CONTINUALLY."

> ➢ Job protected his sons through early Morning Prayer.
> ➢ Job interceded for his children every morning.
> ➢ We are Job.
> ➢ We need to protect our spiritual sons in the early Morning Prayer.

DAVID KNEW HOW TO WORSHIP IN THE MORNING

Psalm 59:16 *"BUT I WILL SING OF THY POWER; YEA, I WILL SING ALOUD OF THY MERCY IN THE MORNING: FOUR THOU HAST BEEN MY DEFENSE AND REFUGE IN THE DAY OF MY TROUBLE."*

GOD SPEAKS IN THE MORNING

Ezekiel 12:8 *"AND IN THE MORNING CAME THE WORD OF THE LORD UNTO ME, SAYING,..."*

If you seek Him in the morning, God answers.

NEW LIFE CAME IN THE MORNING

Mark 16:9a *"NOW WHEN JESUS WAS RISEN EARLY THE FIRST DAY OF THE WEEK,..."*

If Jesus resurrected in the morning, that tells us that the new lives that God has already prepared are won over through that early Morning Prayer.

THE BRIGHT AND MORNING STAR

Revelation 22:16 *"I JESUS HAVE SENT MINE ANGEL TO TESTIFY UNTO YOU THESE THINGS IN THE CHURCHES. I AM THE ROOT AND THE OFFSPRING OF DAVID, AND THE BRIGHT AND MORNING STAR."*

There are stars that come out at night and there are daystars that come out in the morning. It's the shining bright morning star that only comes out in the morning. If Jesus is that star we need to seek Him in the mornings.

CONCLUSION

It's necessary for every believer to be a man or woman of prayer. But it's best to pray in the morning. If we want to gather the harvest that God already has prepared we must pray in the morning. If we want to apply Vision Crece it's necessary to understand early Morning Prayer. Early morning prayer goes hand in hand with the family altar; since it's in that prayer we'll be interceding for the list of people that we will be winning or have won for the kingdom of heaven.

I encourage you to be one of the ones whom God places a burden on to intercede for the rest. I declare that those who understand what early Morning Prayer is will be risen up by the Holy Ghost to pray in the morning to intercede one for another.

Blessings.

CHAPTER V

DISCIPLE OR CHRISTIAN?

In this chapter I'm going to speak on some biblical truths that few dare to speak about. You don't need to be in agreement with me. The truth is that whatever I have to say about it is not important, but what the Bible has to say is important. It may clash with your theology, your doctrine, or your belief system. The only thing I want is for you to understand the spirit in which the words that the apostles spoke to the primitive church. After all, they are the example we are to follow.

Romans 12:2 *"AND BE NOT CONFORMED TO THIS WORLD: BUT BE YE TRANSFORMED BY THE RENEWING OF YOUR MIND, THAT YE MAY PROVE WHAT IS THAT GOOD, AND ACCEPTABLE, AND PERFECT, WILL OF GOD,"*

The Apostle Paul is saying that it is necessary to renew our understanding and today you are acquiring revelation from God. It's up to you if you can renew the way you think or if you will be satisfied with what you already know.

THE LANGUAGE OF THE PRIMITIVE CHURCH

Acts 2:44 *"AND ALL THAT BELIEVED WERE TOGETHER, AND HAD ALL THINGS COMMON;"*

Let me explain the context of this verse so we can understand it. Chapter 2 of the book of Acts tells us about the coming of the Holy Ghost. From verse 14 on, we find the first message from Peter to the multitudes. In Verse 37 the multitudes recognize their error and they ask Peter and the apostles, what do we do? It's a very open ended question.

What do we do for what? To be saved? To be like you? To be from the way? To be a Christian? Or to be disciples? In verse 38 Peter answers them. He tells them to repent and be baptized in the name of Jesus Christ for the remission of their sins. In verse 41, 3,000 were baptized. This was the first group who was baptized after the 120 had received the gift of the Holy Ghost on the day of Pentecost.

Now we are in verse 42. Those 3,000 remained in the doctrine of the apostles, in communion one with another, and in prayer. What I want you to understand is that this was the first batch of those who had been baptized.

Acts 4:32 *"AND THE MULTITUDE OF THEM THAT BELIEVED WERE OF ONE HEART AND OF ONE SOUL: NEITHER SAID ANY OF THEM THAT OUGHT OF THE THINGS WHICH HE*

POSSESSED WAS HIS OWN; BUT THEY HAD ALL THINGS COMMON."

In this verse it keeps telling us about this first group of the baptized. They continued together. They still don't have a label.

Acts 6:1a *"AND IN THOSE DAYS, WHEN THE NUMBER OF THE DISCIPLES WAS MULTIPLIED, THERE AROSE A MURMURING OF THE GRECIANS AGAINST THE HEBREWS...."*

Acts 6:2a *"THEN THE TWELVE CALLED THE MULTITUDE OF THE DISCIPLES UNTO THEM, AND SAID..."*

NOTE: This multitude is the same 3000 and more that have been added up unto that point. Also note the following, now they are being called DISCIPLES. This first multitude of believers is known now as DISCIPLES. So every believer is a DISCIPLE. This is what the Bible says, if you are a believer then you are a DISCIPLE.

Acts 6:7 *"AND THE WORD OF GOD INCREASED; AND THE NUMBER OF THE DISCIPLES MULTIPLIED IN JERUSALEM GREATLY; AND A GREAT COMPANY OF THE PRIESTS WERE OBEDIENT TO THE FAITH."*

THE DISCIPLES continued to grow according to the word they preached. Why did the apostles call these first believers disciples? Because Jesus had given them the command to go and make DISCIPLES of all nations. Jesus did not tell them to make Christians, rather DISCIPLES. This is why the apostles called this first group of believers, DISCIPLES. So up unto this point all who believed in Jesus were called DISCIPLES.

Acts 11:26 *"AND WHEN HE HAD FOUND HIM, HE BROUGHT HIM UNTO ANTIOCH. AND IT CAME TO PASS, THAT A WHOLE YEAR THEY ASSEMBLED THEMSELVES WITH THE CHURCH, AND TAUGHT MUCH PEOPLE. AND THE DISCIPLES WERE CALLED CHRISTIANS FIRST IN ANTIOCH."*

From chapter 11 of the book of Acts their name is changed from disciples to Christians. Note the following: it was not the apostles who changed their name. Neither was it the Holy Ghost who had revealed it to them. No. It was an idea that the unbelievers had. These were not disciples. They had found a way to mock the disciples. In other words, because some heathen want to call us what they want to call us, we believe it.

Nowadays the majority knows us as Christians and not that it's all bad for us to be called that. I'll explain that further on. Jesus gave the apostles an order in Matthew 28:19, *"GO YE THEREFORE, AND MAKE DISCIPLES...."* (ASV) The command is clear.

The order that Jesus gave is to go and make disciples: not to make Christians.

So now it seems as though we have paid more mind to the sons of the devil than to the apostles and Jesus himself. There's a notable difference in having a disciple's mentality and one of a Christian. I want us to understand that Jesus gave the command to make disciples, and the apostles obeyed Him.

There's not an exact date of when the book of Acts was written. It's believed that it was written between the 70s and 90s of the first century although there are some historical evidences that don't match. What is certain is that approximately around this date the persecution of the disciples began and they were scattered all about.

In the 200s and the early 300s there were very few disciples and the few that existed were now called Christians in order to identify and kill them. Eusebius, one of the church historians of these first centuries, in one of his books tells us that in approximately 306, Constantine named himself the emperor of the western empire.

The historian tells us that Constantine had seen a sign in which he saw the figure of a cross, with an inscription that read "Conquer by this". Afterwards Constantine tells of how he had a dream in which Christ tells him to make a military banner in the form of a cross and this standard would give him protection in all battles. At any rate after the emperor began to win many battles he began to give great force to Christianity. This Roman Emperor, in conjunction with the then Catholic

Church, began to take force beginning in the year 325 on.

In the late 1500s and early 1600s Martin Luther begins a protest against the Catholic Church. With this act the protestant church is born. Out of this move we find the Lutherans, the Presbyterians, Methodists, Baptists, Assemblies of God, and countless others. We know them all as Christians. All of these denominations have their roots with Martin Luther and his wanting to reform the Catholic Church. Since then we all continue to drag with us the label of Christians. The true name that began in the primitive church was lost since the first centuries.

We know that God is restoring all things and that the true name his followers have is the same one Jesus himself commanded of the apostles to make: DISCIPLES.

Now where then did we get the name of CHRISTIANS? If we understand the true meaning of the word Christian then we know it's not all bad to be known as such. But the truth is few know why we are called Christians. CHRISTIANS comes from the word CHRIST.

CHRIST - from the Greek CHRISTOS = ANOINTED
CHRIST - from the Hebrew MASHIACH = ANOINTED
CHRISTIAN - from the Greek CHRISTIANOS = LITTLE CHRISTS

So if they call us CHRISTIANS because we are small Christs' or anointed ones, then great. But you and I know that we are not called CHRISTIANS because we are anointed or because we are small Christs'. In fact, if someone were to say they are a small Christ it would be a blasphemy. If you call someone the anointed one, it's criticized. The truth is we ignore the true meaning of the words. Jesus knew all these things hence He says go and make disciples.

Acts 14:21 *"AND WHEN THEY HAD PREACHED THE GOSPEL TO THAT CITY, AND HAD MADE MANY DISCIPLES, THEY RETURNED TO LYSTRA, AND TO ICONIUM, AND TO ANTIOCH,"* (ASV)

Pay attention to what the bible passage states about MAKING many disciples. Disciples are MADE. They're FORMED. CHRISTIANS are just invited to accept Christ and they are set on a pew of a church. Making a disciple requires conversion. Forming him is an entire process.

A disciple is: formed, broken, transformed, and processed until he attains perfection. A disciple never stops learning.

Luke 6:40 *"THE DISCIPLE IS NOT ABOVE HIS MASTER: BUT EVERY ONE THAT IS PERFECT SHALL BE AS HIS MASTER."*

Every disciple has a master to whom he renders accounts. A Christian doesn't want to submit to any authority. The final objective is to be equal to the master and a disciple can even do greater things. Yet that does not make him greater than his master. Jesus said, "Greater things than these shall you do." But that will never make us greater than Jesus.

Matthew 28:20 *"TEACHING THEM TO OBSERVE ALL THINGS WHATSOEVER I HAVE COMMANDED YOU: AND, LO, I AM WITH YOU ALWAYS, EVEN UNTO THE END OF THE WORLD. AMEN."*

In verse 19 of the same chapter Jesus has given the command to GO and MAKE disciples. In the 20th verse Jesus is saying that these same disciples *should be taught to keep all the things He had taught them.* The command is to make disciples, then bring them to church. The church is comprised of disciples.

Today a pastor will be raised up and the first thing he wants to do is find a building. He doesn't want to make disciples. Things are being done in reverse. That's why church isn't "working."

THE FIVEFOLD MINISTRY

Ephesians 4:11-12 *"AND HE GAVE SOME, APOSTLES; AND SOME, PROPHETS; AND SOME, EVANGELISTS; AND SOME, PASTORS AND TEACHERS; FOR THE PERFECTING OF THE SAINTS, FOR THE WORK OF THE MINISTRY, FOR THE EDIFYING OF THE BODY OF CHRIST:"*

If Jesus put in His church these five ministries, it was for a purpose. That purpose is so that the apostles, prophets, evangelists, pastors, and teachers be in charge of perfecting the saints. The work is not just of the pastors, evangelists, or the teachers. It belongs to all five. If a church does not believe in apostles and prophets and they function only with evangelists, pastors, and teachers, then that church is incomplete. The result is that the members are not being perfected.

So a disciple should pass through a process towards perfection.

THE DISCIPLES OF JESUS

Luke 6:13 *"AND WHEN IT WAS DAY, HE CALLED UNTO HIM HIS DISCIPLES: AND OF THEM HE CHOSE TWELVE, WHOM ALSO HE NAMED APOSTLES;"*

Jesus did not call them Christian followers. He called them disciples. He had many disciples and from these He chose twelve and called those Apostles.

Luke 14:26 *"IF ANY MAN COME TO ME, AND HATE NOT HIS FATHER, AND MOTHER, AND WIFE, AND CHILDREN, AND BRETHREN, AND SISTER, YA, AND HIS OWN LIFE ALSO, HE CANNOT BE MY DISCIPLE."*

He's not telling us to curse our parents, spouse, sons, or brethren. That would be contrary to the scriptures. What Jesus is saying is that He is first and before all things. Jesus is teaching priorities. He must be first before your husband, wife, brethren, and the rest of your relatives. He must even be above your personal desires.

CONCLUSION

To end this chapter, it's necessary to understand what it is that Jesus said as well as what the apostles practiced at the beginning of the church of the Lord Jesus Christ. It's a question of getting used to the biblical language and not what religion has taught us. You decide whether to obey religion or what Jesus said regarding going and making disciples.

PART TWO

CHAPTER VI

THE GREAT COMMANDMENT

Matthew 28:18-20 *"AND JESUS CAME TO THEM AND SPAKE UNTO THEM, SAYING, ALL AUTHORITY HATH BEEN GIVEN UNTO ME IN HEAVEN AND ON EARTH. GO YE THEREFORE, AND MAKE DISCIPLES OF ALL THE NATIONS, BAPTIZING THEM INTO THE NAME OF THE FATHER AND OF THE SON AND OF THE HOLY SPIRIT: TEACHING THEM TO OBSERVE ALL THINGS WHATSOEVER I COMMANDED YOU: AND LO, I AM WITH YOU ALWAYS, EVEN UNTO THE END OF THE WORLD."*

THE GREAT COMMANDMENT

Jesus, after having taught his disciples for approximately three years and a half, gives them a command. Note one very important detail, Jesus did not give this command to his students until He saw they were ready. With this mandate He ended His earthly ministry. The success of the mission was contingent on this command. Everything that Jesus taught during these three years is in the hands of those that receive this commission and they're ability to fulfill it to the letter. The work that Jesus had done with the disciples would mean nothing if they don't realize this work. Now the disciples by this time already healed sick, delivered captives, raised the lame, etc. They were now ready to go on to the next level. They had been taught, enabled, prepared, and readied to fulfill the great commission.

This mandate is still valid today. It was not only for those first disciples. It is for today's disciples as well. The problem is that this command is being forgotten and is not being practiced in many churches, generally speaking.

It's necessary to restore the command that Jesus gave His disciples before parting. To comply with this command we must have a disciple's mentality as opposed to a Christian one. It's much easier to be a Christian than to be a disciple, hence we more often hear the word Christian than disciple. To be a Christian all is needed is for you to go to church, and well, now you're a Christian. On the contrary, to be a disciple you must believe in the Lord Jesus Christ as your savior, be baptized and die to yourself in order to submit to the authority God gives you as a covering.

If we pay attention to verses 19 and 20 we find enclosed all the work that Jesus did with His disciples. Jesus begins by telling them in verse 18 that all power was given to Him in Heaven and in Earth. These words could not have been said by Jesus before He had been dead and resurrected. Before He had died and resurrected, He had authority in the earth, but not in the heavens. Because up until then Jesus had acted simply as a man. It wasn't until He had resurrected that God had made Him both Lord AND Christ.

Jesus says; by the authority that has now been conferred to me I now give you an order. And that order is found in verse 19: "Go!" If we look at the verb "Go", it's an imperative tense. This means that the command continues on today.

When a command is given in imperative tense it means the command is ongoing. Jesus gives the order to "GO" so that we go today, tomorrow, and we must continue to go. Jesus said go and make, both words are in the same tense. So then, this command is still valid today. Unfortunately, many churches are not fulfilling this command.

Note that again the order is to make disciples and not Christians. Today we justify ourselves by making Christians. To be a Christian all that is needed is to gather in a temple and that makes you a Christian, even if you've never had an experience with God. But to make a disciple requires great investment, effort, dedication, work, and time. This is what Jesus did with His disciples. We don't want to pay the price as Jesus did.

Church, we must restore this great command and begin to preach to the Christians so that we may begin to make disciples and thus fulfill this command.

WHAT DO WE DO WITH DISCIPLES?

The commandment here is to baptize the disciples. How? In the name of the Father, and of the Son, and of the Holy Spirit.

Allow me to make a small parenthesis and speak about baptism since it is part of this commandment given by Jesus Christ. Just as we haven't obeyed the commandment to GO and MAKE, we have also not obeyed correctly the commandment of baptism.

FIRST: Father, Son, and Holy Spirit are not proper names. Until today, I know not one parent who has named their son "Holy Spirit" or that would say your name is "Father" or "Son." Why? Because Father, Son, and Holy Spirit are not names.

SECOND: The commandment is that we baptize them "IN THE NAME." Note that it says "IN THE NAME." It does not say IN THE NAMES. It's singular and not plural.

THIRD: The commandment is given to the disciples, and they in ACTS 2:38 fulfilled it. The disciples knew what that Name was and they executed the order.

EXAMPLE: If your boss gives you the order: "Bring me a glass of water." What do you do to execute the order? Well, you bring him the glass of water and it's as simple as that. But what would happen if instead of bringing the water, you simply say, "Bring me a glass of water?" What would you be doing? Repeating the order. But, you wouldn't be obeying it.

This is what's happening in the majority of Christianity. The order is only being repeated. When someone is baptizing saying "in the Name of the Father, Son, and Holy Spirit", they are repeating the order but they are not fulfilling it.

Church, everything that is not being done according to the original design of God must be restored. If you have understood this explanation of baptism, I tell you as Silas told Paul. What are you waiting for? Get up! Wash away your sins calling upon the Name of the Lord Jesus Christ. Now I close the baptism parentheses.

FOUR WORDS

If we observe this command well, the church in general hasn't been carrying it out. They are not going, nor are they making disciples, or baptizing them correctly. That's why the condition of the church throughout the entire world is in a spiritually poor state. It's necessary to return to the times of Jesus and take again the order that He left us before parting.

During the three years that Jesus carried out His ministry he realized an excellent work with His disciples. In fact, the order that He left us is what He had done throughout the three years He was with them. All the work that Jesus did in that time frame can be summarized in four words:

1. Evangelize
2. Consolidate
3. Disciple

4. Send

In these four words are encapsulated all the work that Jesus wants His church to realize. These four words fit within the great commission.

EVANGELIZE

The word evangelize comes from the same word for GOSPEL and the word gospel is not a religious one as many of us know it today. This word was quite common in Jesus's time on the earth.

GOSPEL = good news.

What is good news? Everything that sounds good to you is good news. If someone tells you they are gifting you a new car, that would be considered good news. That is gospel. The word gospel then, is not a religious one. Remove from your mind what religion has inculcated in you.

EVANGELIZE = to notify of some good news.

EVANGELIZE = the act of speaking or teaching all you know.

In this case to evangelize is to share with someone all that you have believed. We have all one way or another evangelized someone. What we must learn is to do it as Jesus did it and put it into practice in order to obtain the results He had.

CONSOLIDATION

CONSOLIDATION = to give firmness, security, and solidity to something or someone. The act of consolidation is the most important of all four, since we all in one way or another evangelize or disciple. Once the newly converted person is sharing what they've learned, they've been sent. But consolidation is the act of giving firmness, security, and solidity to that new believer.

CONSOLIDATE = Retention of the newly converted in the church and body of Christ.

Most churches go from event to event trying to win souls to Christ, but most of these are sterile methods. They'll plan a great evangelistic campaign in order to add souls to the church, and the idea is not a bad one, per se, but thousands of dollars are wasted to carry out the event for 5,000 souls but most of the attendees are already saved Christians. In the end of those that attended 100 answer the call to accept Jesus Christ as their savior and of those 100, given three or four months turn into only ten left.

What happened to the other ninety people that accepted Jesus as savior? They were lost. They returned to their way of life: to the world again. Why? It was due to the lack of consolidation.

The only thing the church has done is win these converts and then sit them down in the pews of the church and let the Holy Ghost take care of them. What the church has not understood is that to win souls unto the kingdom of heaven is warfare. If you don't consolidate, the enemy will make them fall into temptation so that they return to sin again.

Further ahead I'll get deeper into the topic of consolidation for the souls.

DISCIPLE

DISCIPLE = to teach a believer everything you know and believe

Matthew 28:20: *"TEACHING THEM TO OBSERVE ALL THINGS WHATSOEVER I HAVE COMMANDED YOU:"*

After you have evangelized them, they converted to Christ, and you consolidated them, we then need to teach them all that He commanded. This is what Jesus was doing with His disciples during three years He walked with them. This is discipleship.

SEND

SEND = the action of putting into practice all that you learned throughout the first three actions; it's for the disciple to put into practice everything he learned in the acts of evangelism, consolidation, and discipling; in other words he will evangelize just as he was evangelized; consolidate as he was consolidated; disciple as he was discipled.

When this disciple puts into practice all that he learned it's because he's been sent. This is what Jesus did with His disciples after the three years He carried out his ministry. This is the mandate He left us; to do what he did on the Earth.

If the church could understand that in this commission is the secret of winning the world for Christ. I believe we would all be doing it. Remember that we must evangelize, consolidate, disciple, and send the new believers to begin to dominate the systems that control the world.

CONCLUSION

Everything not being done according to what Jesus did must be restored. It's never too late to begin. I encourage you, who are reading this book, Vision Crece, if you are one of the ones who have not obeyed the mandate in its totality, that you would ask forgiveness from the Lord Jesus Christ and align yourself with this truth.

In the Name of the Lord Jesus Christ I declare that you be an instrument in Hands of the Holy Spirit that will begin to gather the end time harvest.

CHAPTER VII

COMPASSION FOR SOULS

Luke 2:49 *"AND HE SAID UNTO THEM, HOW IS IT THAT YE SOUGHT ME? WIST YE NOT THAT I MUST BE ABOUT MY FATHER'S BUSINESS?"*

Jesus knew His purpose since childhood. He knew His calling was for souls. He knew He had been sent to save souls. This is why when His parents looked for Him and they found Him in the temple with the teachers of the law, His mother asked, "Why did you do this to us? His answer was that He must be about His Father's business. Jesus knew His purpose here on earth. He had it very clear. Jesus did not even allow for his parents to interfere in the business for which His Father had sent Him.

We all know that Jesus established His kingdom in the earth and in order to expand said kingdom we need souls. This is why Jesus knew that He first must save souls in order to fulfill His purpose.

Let's notice that Jesus used the word BUSINESS in referring to His purpose.

LET'S ANALYZE A BUSINESS

Every businessman or any business owner knows that the success of his business is not contingent on his investment, nor his publicity, or from customer service, or from any other necessary thing that is also necessary for a successful business. Rather, there is one very important factor and Jesus carried it out as He began His ministry. The success of every business depends on the training of all employees.

As an example, let's say next Sunday a fast food restaurant is opening, The owner knows that at the very least two weeks prior, he has to train the employees so that at opening time they already know what they are to do in their respective departments. For this, he hires someone with managerial experience in that sector and that individual is in charge of training and preparing the employees. Two weeks before opening day, the employees are already making a paycheck and the owner does not care about the cost to him during this training time because he knows it's part of the investment he must make for the success of his business. The owner knows that the success of his business hangs on the good training of his employees and the trustworthiness of his manager. It would seem as if the owner is losing money since he is paying a wage before there is any income, but he knows he is not. It's a part of the investment for a successful business.

SOUL BUSINESS

Jesus knew about this business principle. That's why when He began His ministry, the first thing He did was choose His disciples and trained and equipped them for three years. Jesus knew that the good success of His purpose depended on the equipping and training of His disciples.

Jesus did not care that it took three years to train his disciples. He knew that the success of the commission to GO and DISCIPLE hinged on the well equipping and training that they would receive during their time with Him.

How great was this equipping and training that the disciples received that, thanks to it we continue this day to speak of the savior of the world! The main purpose of Jesus today for us on the earth is that we expand the kingdom of heaven. In order to fulfill this work we need well equipped and trained disciples that would die to themselves and fulfill the vision of the kingdom of heaven. For the fulfillment of this vision we need the same compassion for souls that Jesus had.

Matthew 9:36 *"BUT WHEN HE SAW THE MULTITUDES, HE WAS MOVED WITH COMPASSION ON THEM, BECAUSE THEY FAINTED, AND WERE SCATTERED ABROAD, AS SHEEP HAVING NO SHEPHERD."*

A lamb with no shepherd is a destitute lamb therefore she suffers pain, sadness, fear, and is in danger that a wolf could cause her harm or kill her. Jesus understood all of the dangers that these souls were prone to and the sufferings they had. That's why it says He was moved with COMPASSION for these souls.

In order to apply Vision Crece, it's necessary that the disciples in training would have compassion and not just passion for souls. Although passion is good, compassion reaches further.

COMPASSION VS PASSION

PASSION = A feeling that is so strong it's able to dominate your will through what you like: love, jealousy, wrath, hatred, etc.

COMPASSION = A feeling of sadness, suffering, and pain that we feel when we see someone else suffer that impulses us to heal the hurt, suffering, or pain or help avoid it. There then exists a marked difference:

PASSION
- Leads you to satisfying yourself while compassion leads to satisfying your neighbor.
- Leads you to commit acts you will feel remorse over later.
- Is selfish: makes you think only of yourself.
- Damages, destroys, and kills.
- Blinds you.
- Brings violence.

COMPASSION
* Leads you to commit acts that leave you feeling fulfilled and content.
* Leads to selflessness and solidarity.
* Helps, Restores, and gives life.
* Brings unification.
* Gives love.
* Suffers with those who suffer.
* Weeps with those who weep.
* Feels his neighbor's pain.
* Goes further than passion.

This is why Jesus had compassion for the souls when he saw them abandoned and without a spiritual father to tend to them.

COMPASSION GIVES YOU THE STRENGTH TO TRIUMPH

A person full of compassion is unstoppable. There exists nothing in life that stops someone full of compassion.

Jesus was full of compassion and this is why nothing or nobody could have stopped the purpose for which Jesus was on the earth. The disciples were full of compassion. That's why, even though they suffered many things: lashings, imprisonment, shipwrecks, snakebites, persecution, etc., nothing could stop them; not even death itself could. Why then do we continue to talk about them after their deaths? What gave them the strength to continue onward and fulfill their calling? It was the compassion they felt for the souls.

Compassion is like gasoline for your engine. Without the gasoline you will go nowhere. But with a tank full of gas you will be able to go far. Compassion is the strength of your calling. The devil is not interested in your calling. He is interested in removing the compassion that God placed within your calling; because he knows that without compassion you will not fulfill said calling.

If someone has a calling from God they should also have compassion and if they don't have compassion in their calling, it's not from God. It was God who placed compassion in His Son Jesus for the souls. Nobody can have compassion in and of themselves unless God gives it. Let's ask the Father that He would give us compassion for souls and in that way apply Vision Crece.

Vision Crece is about the business of God here on the earth, and it's gathering the harvest of souls that He already has for each ministry. But it has not manifested in all because there are still too few laborers to carry out the mission. I invite you to be one of those disciples that God is preparing so that you can fulfill the great commission that Jesus gave us before he left to GO and MAKE disciples in all the "cosmos".

CONCLUSION

I declare that you, who is reading this book, will be of the warriors that God is equipping and depositing in you compassion for souls so that you would feel what Jesus felt as He was dying on the cross for each and every one of them.

CHAPTER VIII

CONSOLIDATION

CONSOLIDATION = The action of giving firmness, solidity, or establishing someone or something

Jesus evangelized His disciples at the moment He called them and told them to follow Him. He consolidated them when He didn't leave them alone from the time they accepted: in this way He taught them all they should do. He sent them at the moment He told them to put into practice all they had learned.

At the moment that you speak with someone about what Christ has done in your life, or you invite them to church, you're evangelizing. We've disciple them by teaching them all we know. Once he has now learned some of what we taught him and puts it into practice with his relatives or friends, he is sent.

We normally do these three actions without knowing or at least without any specific planning.

CONSOLIDATION

But what I want to speak to you about in this chapter is about consolidation, since most churches aren't practicing it.

Of the four actions already mentioned, I consider consolidation as the most important. The retention of souls in the body of Christ depends on it. The majority of churches have events in order to reach souls but there is no plan for retention.

As an example, one church makes an event geared for five thousand souls. Tremendous amounts of money are spent, and it's not a bad thing to invest in souls; the problem is that in the end, if we analyze the results, it was more noise we made than actually saving the souls. If five thousand went, and out of those one thousand accepted Jesus Christ as savior, in about six or ten months' time, of those one thousand souls only one hundred are left. In one more year, there will only be ten.

The problem is not that the souls are hard. No, because we can see the results. It was one thousand that accepted Christ as their savior. The problem is that most churches just don't have a retention plan for these souls. This is called consolidation. It's better to have a vision to follow than to be shadowboxing. I can win ten souls for Christ on the street without the big noise or huge money investment.

Consolidation comes into play at the same moment that a soul receives Jesus as savior. From that very moment, the person that spoke to them about Christ takes charge of continuing with follow-up for this newborn baby. The new birth is warfare in the spiritual realm and if the person that spoke to them does not know this, the babe will be lost. Every person that has not accepted Jesus as savior is under the influence of the kingdom of darkness and at the moment that that person accepts Jesus, a struggle begins for his soul. The devil will not easily release someone who belonged to him. That's why it is necessary for the baby to receive all the necessary attentions given to a newborn.

He is a newly born baby and if the first three days are not used to tend to them, then the devil will lead him right back out into the world. It's absolutely vital that we understand how important consolidation is and that it is fundamental to the life of every newborn.

APPLYING CONSOLIDATION

To apply consolidation it's necessary for disciples to be well trained in what consolidation is. Consolidation is to make yourself the newborn babe's shadow. It's to take care of the baby: feed him, change him, care for him, protect him, or tend to him. Remember that they will be under enemy attack. Do not leave them alone. Don't be careless with them. Pray with them. Pray for them.

Think for a moment that when a baby is born in a hospital there is so much attention that the baby needs and how personnel are mobilized. That baby unknowingly is being cared for. The doctors know that the first three days after birth are crucial for the healthy development of that baby. Nurses tend to him. Different specialists in their fields check all of the baby's systems: is he breathing normally, eating normally, they check from head to toe. They are assured the baby is complete or deformed. The baby is fed every three hours. The healthy growth of the baby is contingent on the attention he receives during those first three days. This is the same attention that the recent convert needs.

We are those nurses, doctors, and specialists in charge of tending to the newborn. From the very moment that that person accepts Christ as savior, that baby then comes to be our responsibility and must be taken care of. Never leave him alone otherwise relatives and friends who don't know Jesus will begin to attack him. He doesn't know how to defend himself yet. That baby needs our care.

Call them at morning, noon, and night. We will gift them a book called "My Connection With God." You maintain contact through phone calls, text messages, taking them to lunch or to a cup of coffee. You become their shadow until they stand firm and are convinced they are in the right place.

After that first week we will give them a copy of the book D.B.H. School, where we will also be following up with them after every lesson. The book consists of seven studies on Deliverance, seven on Blessing, and seven on Healing. During these twenty one days we will be guiding them with these lessons. Remember that this baby has just been born and is now in a war and if you leave him alone, the devil will snatch him from your hands. Now, Jesus has already done the work in him because he is already saved. Now it's up to you to tend to him, and one day God will ask us to give an account.

This is the problem of most churches in that they don't want to struggle with souls. We want our temples to be filled with them, but we don't want to work to retain them. That's why the commandment of Jesus before he parted was that we would make disciples and not Christians. A Christian just sits on the pew and is fed and a disciple feeds others. Nowadays we have buildings full of Christians and very few disciples and in order to carry out consolidation we need to have a disciple mentality as opposed to a Christian one.

This is why we've been losing the harvest: due to the lack of disciples willing to sacrifice themselves for souls. Anyone can be a Christian, but not just anyone can be a good disciple and in order to apply Vision Crece we need to have a disciple's mentality.

Consolidation requires effort, sacrifice, dedication, and investment. Above all, that you would be full of compassion for souls. Consolidation within the great commission and Vision Crece is of high importance. If we want to gather the soul harvest it's necessary to correctly apply consolidation.

There are too many already saved souls that are being lost due to the lack of someone who will care for them. We want the Holy Ghost to take charge of taking care of them and we are happy just sitting them in the church pew, waiting for them to grow when no one will check on them.

Vision Crece comes from the heart of God to avoid this type of error and no longer lose souls. Jesus said in John 18:9b, *"OF THEM WHICH THOU GAVEST ME HAVE I LOST NONE."* If Jesus declared that He lost no one, this then is an example to follow. Jesus did not allow for any to be lost.

The truth is that the modern day church has been negligent in our relationship to souls.

CONCLUSION

The church needs to recognize that we are not doing things as He wants us to do them. We are losing too many souls after Jesus saves them due to our negligence. It's time to do things as Jesus did when He was walking the earth. Let's not allow the devil to continue stealing from us the souls that already belong to the body of Christ. Let us learn to apply Vision Crece and consolidation in order to disallow more souls to be lost.

I declare that you will be an expert in the consolidation of souls and you will have the necessary compassion to carry out Vision Crece.

CHAPTER IX

CREATED TO BE FRUITFUL

Man as a species was made by God to be fruitful in every area of life. Not only in the reproduction aspect.

Genesis 1:28 *"AND GOD BLESSED THEM, AND GOD SAID UNTO THEM, BE FRUITFUL, AND MULTIPLY, AND REPLENISH THE EARTH, AND SUBDUE IT: AND HAVE DOMINION OVER THE FISH OF THE SEA, AND OVER THE FOWL OF THE AIR, AND OVER EVERY LIVING THING THAT MOVETH UPON THE EARTH."*

Note that God, immediately after He blessed him, gave the command, BE FRUITFUL AND MULTIPLY. God knew the importance of fruitfulness and that's why the first thing He did was bless them. We have already been blessed to produce fruit.

Let's look at something that is very important. Everything that God is doing in verses 26-28 is in the spiritual realm and not the natural. If we read Genesis 2:7, we will find out that not until then did God form man out of the dust of the earth and in Genesis 1:27 God created man as a spirit.

The word used in Gen. 1:27 where it says "GOD CREATED MAN," is the word "BARA." It means "to create something out of nothing." The word used in Gen. 2:7 where it says, "THE LORD GOD FORMED MAN OF THE DUST OF THE GROUND.." the word there is "YATSAR" which means "to mold."

BARA= TO CREATE SOMETHING OUT OF NOTHING

YATSAR= TO MOLD, TO FORM

The man as a specie was created in the spiritual and formed in the natural. We then have two natures: spiritual and physical. We have two needs: spiritual and natural. We have two deaths: spiritual and physical. The apostle Paul says in Ephesians 2:10 that we were CREATED in Christ Jesus.

I explain all this so we can understand that when God says to be fruitful, he's speaking in the spiritual, since man had not yet been formed. Now everything in the spiritual has a physical reflection. The fruitfulness can also be seen in the natural.

The word that God uses for BE FRUITFUL is "PARA", which means FERTILE. The word used by MULTIPLY is "RABA: which means to AUGMENT and ABUNDANCE.

This same order God established in Geneses 1:22 to all fish, fowl, beast and plants. The design of God for His creation is that we would produce much fruit, in the spiritual as well as the natural. Since all truth is parallel, it is also reflected in the physical.

John 15:5 *"I AM THE VINE, YE ARE THE BRANCHES: HE THAT ABIDETH IN ME, AND I IN HIM, THE SAME BRINGETH FORTH MUCH FRUIT: FOR WITHOUT ME YE CAN DO NOTHING."*

Jesus is saying that He is the vine and we are the branches where the grapes grow. The branches depend on the vine in order to produce grapes. The function of the branch is to produce leaves and fruit but it has to stay connected to the vine. There's no need for invention. We need to stay connected to Jesus to produce fruit. If we are not producing fruit, then we are only full of leaves and the Bible states that we will be known by our fruits. It does not say that we will be known by the leaves. Nowadays there are many leafy Christians but the fruit is lacking and God blessed us to be fruitful.

John 15:8 *"HEREIN IS MY FATHER GLORIFIED, THAT YE BEAR MUCH FRUIT; SO SHALL YE BE MY DISCIPLES."*

If we want to glorify our Father, we must give much fruit. Look what the Apostle John says. We must not only give fruit, but much fruit. It's the nature that God gave us to produce much fruit. It continues to say. *"SO SHALL YE BE MY DISCIPLES."* John says that in order to be disciples we need to produce much fruit. In other words, those of us that have a disciple's mentality will produce much fruit.

There's no such thing as someone saying, "I'm a disciple," while having no fruits, because disciples are recognized by their fruits. Now we speak of fruit in every area of our lives: fruits in our spiritual life, marriage, finances, career, etc. Above all in soul winning for the kingdom of heaven.

SIN TOOK OUR FRUITFULNESS AWAY

Romans 7:4 *"WHEREFORE, MY BRETHREN, YE ALSO ARE BECOME DEAD TO THE LAW BY THE BODY OF CHRIST; THAT YE SHOULD BE MARRIED TO ANOTHER, EVEN TO HIM WHO IS RAISED FROM THE DEAD, THAT WE SHOULD BRING FORTH FRUIT UNTO GOD."*

The Apostle Paul is telling us we have died to the law of sin. That law is the one that took fruitfulness away from us. Remember that God blessed us to be fruitful but when Adam sinned, we entered into the law of sin and it removed that blessing. But, here the Apostle Paul is telling us we have died to that law of sin and if we are dead to it, then we should be producing fruit. All who have died to sin should be fruitful. If someone claims to be a disciple and cannot bear forth fruit in any area of their life then they have not yet died to sin.

GOD IS A GOD OF PRINCIPLES

If God is a God of principles, then He is not moved by the people's emotions. For example, if a

Christian is unfaithful in his offerings, tithes, and first fruits, then God cannot bless him with the blessings that are loosed with offerings, tithes, and first fruits. Even if you cry, pray, and fast for forty days for God's blessings, He will not because He established a principle in His word He will not violate.

God said, "Honor your father and mother that it may go well with you and you may have long life, and even if you pray, fast, preach, speak in tongues, and do all you want, but dishonor your parents, it will go badly for you and you will die sooner than you should.

That's how God works. He is a God of principles and if we don't understand this, we can spend all of our life in the house of God waiting for His blessings. I will die without being able to fulfill the purpose for which I'm on the earth.

If one of the principles God set is that you and I produce much fruit once we are dead to sin and we aren't, then we haven't completely died to sin.

We all have the same responsibility facing the great commission to make disciples. That is, we need to give forth much fruit.

STERILITY PRODUCED BY CURSE

Matthew 21:18-19 *"NOW IN THE MORNING AS HE RETURNED INTO THE CITY, HE HUNGERED. AND WHEN HE SAW A FIG TREE IN THE WAY, HE CAME TO IT, AND FOUND NOTHING THEREON, BUT LEAVES ONLY, AND SAID UNTO IT, LET NO FRUIT GROW ON THEE*

HENCEFORWARD FOR EVER. AND PRESENTLY THE FIG TREE WITHERED AWAY."

The first thing we see here is that Jesus cursed the fig tree because of its lack of fruit. This means that if you or I don't begin to give forth fruit, it's possible for a day to come where God will curse us. The word of curse that Jesus released to the fig tree caused it to dry up. If a Christian finds himself in a spiritual drought, discouraged, without a desire to continue, and you feel no more desire for the house of God, then a curse is operating in your life and it's drying you up little by little. The lack of fruit in the child of God produces a spiritual drought. I've always said that the joy a person feels when Jesus is received as savior doesn't compare but with the joy that the same person feels when he wins over someone to Christ.

It's like a mother who just gave birth to a son. The last thing on her mind at that moment is death. All she can think about is life. She's planning her son's life. She's happy, joyous, and content. Everything in that family is happiness. But, what happens if in a marriage there are no children? There's always a sadness among them. They are drying within.

It's the same regarding soul winning. You struggle so that your spiritual son grows healthy and lacking in nothing. That keeps you happy. That keeps you always with a strong spiritual life. But, what happens when a Christian never wins over anyone for Christ? Slowly he begins to spiritually dry up and all due to the lack of a spiritual son for whom to fight for.

It's because our nature is that we are designed to produce much fruit.

We all have the same command to GO and MAKE disciples in every world system that we move in. It's time we fulfill this command. It's time we begin to produce fruit.

CONSEQUENCES OF UNFRUITFULNESS

1 Samuel 1:5-18 *"BUT UNTO HANNAH HE GAVE A WORTHY PORTION; FOR HE LOVED HANNAH: BUT THE LORD HAD SHUT UP HER WOMB. AND HER ADVERSARY ALSO PROVOKED HER SORE, FOR TO MAKE HER FRET, BECAUSE THE LORD HAD SHUT UP HER WOMB. AND AS HE DID SO YEAR BY YEAR, WHEN SHE WENT UP TO THE HOUSE OF THE LORD, SO SHE PROVOKED HER; THEREFORE SHE WEPT, AND DID NOT EAT. THEN SAID ELKANAH HER HUSBAND TO HER, HANNAH, WHY WEEPEST THOU? AND WHY EATEST THOU NOT? AND WHY IS THY HEART GRIEVED? AM I NOT BETTER TO THEE THAN TEN SONS? SO HANNAH ROSE UP AFTER THEY HAD DRUNK. NOW ELI THE PRIEST SAT UPON A SEAT BY A POST OF THE TEMPLE OF THE LORD. AND SHE WAS IN BITTERNESS OF SOUL, AND PRAYED UNTO THE LORD, AND WEPT SORE. AND SHE VOWED A VOW, AND SAID, O LORD OF HOSTS, IF THOU WILT INDEED LOOK*

ON THE AFFLICTION OF THINE HANDMAID, AND REMEMBER ME, AND NOT FORGET THINE HANDMAID, BUT WILT GIVE UNTO THINE HANDMAID A MAN CHILD, THEN I WILL GIVE HIM UNTO THE LORD ALL THE DAYS OF HIS LIFE, AND THERE SHALL NO RAZOR COME UPON HIS HEAD. AND IT CAME TO PASS, AS SHE CONTINUED PRAYING BEFORE THE LORD, THAT ELI MARKED HER MOUTH. NOW HANNAH, SHE SPAKE IN HER HEART; ONLY HER LIPS MOVED, BUT HER VOICE WAS NOT HEARD: THEREFORE ELI THOUGHT SHE HAD BEEN DRUNKEN. AND ELI SAID UNTO HER, HOW LONG WILT THOU BE DRUNKEN? PUT AWAY THY WINE FROM THEE. AND HANNAH ANSWERED AND SAID, NO, MY LORD, I AM A WOMAN OF SORROWFUL SPIRIT: I HAVE DRUNK NEITHER WINE NOR STRONG DRINK, BUT HAVE POURED OUT MY SOUL BEFORE THE LORD. COUNT NOT THINE HANDMAID FOR A DAUGHTER OF BELIAL: FOR OUT OF THE ABUNDANCE OF MY COMPLAINT AND GRIEF HAVE I SPOKEN HITHERTO. THEN ELI ANSWERED AND SAID, GO IN PEACE: AND THE GOD OF ISRAEL GRANT THEE THY PETITION THAT THOU HAST ASKED OF HIM. AND SHE SAID, LET THINE HANDMAID FIND GRACE IN THY SIGHT. SO THE WOMAN WENT HER WAY,

AND DID EAT, AND HER COUNTENANCE WAS NO MORE SAD."

Take note of all the consequences that Hannah was suffering due to the lack of producing fruit:

* IRRITATION
* ANGER
* SADNESS
* WEEPING
* LACK OF APPETITE
* AFFLICTED HEART
* BITTERNESS OF SOUL
* FORGOTTEN
* ABANDONMENT
* REJECTION
* LONELINESS
* CRITICISM
* TRIBULATION
* DISTRESSES

In this story of Hannah we see at least 14 consequences due to not being able to give fruit. Hannah was asking for a biological son and due to not being able to produce fruit she was living these consequences. We know all truth is parallel and everything that happens in the natural happens as well in the spiritual. What happens in the spiritual as well happens in the natural. Therefore, the consequences Hannah suffered for being unfruitful also happens to anyone who is spiritually unfruitful.

This is why we see nowadays that so many of God's children have a burning desire to serve the Lord, but in reality after a little time from conversion, we witness them living the same consequences that Hannah did. There are so many Christians who are sad, afflicted, distressed, bitter, feeling rejected, abandoned, and in a deep loneliness. Even the churches criticize them. That's why they live crying and can't eat. Not because they are fasting, but due to their life condition. All because they have not produced spiritual children. Our nature is fruitful and when we are not giving fruit you become full of these symptoms of frustration and anger.

A FRUITFUL LIFE

When a natural mother has her sons, that mother wants to live and the last thing on her mind is death. When a Christian learns to bring souls into the kingdom he feels alive and the last thing on his mind is backsliding.

Therefore a fruitful life is a life full of happiness, joy, and peace, since you are always occupied tending to your spiritual children. You don't have time for vain distractions. There is no time to waste because a fruitful life will value time. In a fruitful life you stay active in the things of God and don't know discouragement because you always have reason to fight on.

CONCLUSION

Church, it's time that we gather ourselves up from the mediocre condition in which we find ourselves. It's impossible that we would pass all of our lives lamenting about circumstances or fighting each other. God has already blessed us for fruitfulness. There are many people who suffer from sadness and pain. Stop with the excuse that your pastor doesn't teach you anything new. Today there are many sources from which to learn information and if you don't do it for yourself, then it's just an excuse. We have a mandate to fulfill and it's necessary to prepare ourselves. Apply this VISION CRECE manual. Learn as much as you can and let's rescue and retain them in the body of Christ.

CHAPTER X

THE HARVEST IS READY

Just like everything in life, things don't just happen overnight. Everything has its process.

EXAMPLE: If a farmer wants to harvest wheat, he has an entire process to follow before he can harvest wheat.

FIRST: PREPARE THE GROUND. The process of preparing the ground consists of breaking it, combing it, and turning the soil.

SECOND: PLANTING. Afterwards comes the time of sowing. To gather a good harvest you have to select a good seed. It's then deposited into the ground so that it will die and produce new life.

THIRD: WATER THE PLANT. Once the plant has been planted it needs to be watered so that it can develop and give fruit.

FOURTH: CULTIVATE THE PLANT. The process of cultivation consists of placing more soil on the stem so that the roots are very firm.

FIFTH: CARING FOR THE PLANT. The plant needs to be taken care of for a while from the birds for however long necessary until the plant is full grown and firm and the birds aren't able to damage it.

SIXTH: SECOND WATERING SEASON. The plant needs to continue to be watered so that it can grow strong. Certain fertilizers are sometimes added to the water to give more strength to the plant and it can be fruitful.

SEVENTH: PESTICIDES. The function of pesticides is to protect the plant from different plagues, insects, and bugs that can attack it during its development.

EIGHTH: GATHERING THE HARVEST. If the farmer cared for, tended to, and did everything the plant require, he then knows to expect a good harvest.

As we can see in the example of the farmer, in order to gather a harvest, he had to live a long process before he could obtain his reward. This same principle applies to the harvest of souls. The laborer, in this case the farmer. Has to prepare himself in order to gather the harvest of souls applying the same principles if we want that the seed we plant to germinate and produce fruit. We must prepare the land. It's prepared by praying and warring for that land so that when the seed is planted, which is the Word, in that land or person will produce fruit.

Once that person accepts Christ we must water it daily and cultivate it so it won't wither. We do not leave it alone for a moment because a bird can come and eat it. Don't be careless because demons will leave and come back. And if they find the house empty and clean, the demon will enter with seven worse spirits than he.

We must be spraying pesticides so that it will not be plagued. In other words, we must be teaching him what deliverance is so the enemy will not damage him and in that way give the necessary care until he is fully restored.

IS A WAR TO GATHER THE HARVEST

Joel 3:10 *"BEAT YOUR PLOWSHARES INTO SWORDS, AND YOUR PRUNINGHOOKS INTO SPEARS: LET THE WEAK SAY, I AM STRONG."*

If we have just a little knowledge of the tools used for farming, we find out that plowshares and pruninghooks are tools that they used back in those times to work the field, while swords and spears are armaments of war. What the prophet Joel is saying, is that if you've already sowed and used the plowshare and the pruninghook, then now it's time to convert those tools into arms of war: swords and spears. To speak of gathering a harvest is to speak of war. Everything that has to do with planting is war. That's why the devil doesn't let Christians plant money; the universal seed.

Now, if he won't let you plant, much less will he let you harvest; because without sowing, there is no reaping.

What the church doesn't know is that sowing is war. Many Christians sow and never reap because they've never found out that they are in a war. The enemy is going to steal your seed as well as your harvest.

PLOWSHARES AND PRUNINGHOOKS IN HAND

The church in these last days has settled with sowing even if they never harvest. They have been left with plowshares and pruninghooks in their hands without converting them into swords and spears. Church, it makes no sense to gather a harvest. It's a waste of time. If we plant it's because we expect a good and abundant harvest. Don't be left standing with plowshares and pruninghooks in your hands. Beat them into swords and spears because we must fight for the harvest. If we don't, the enemy will take if from us.

We have all, one way or another, planted the Word of God in the people and have settled for that. Maybe it's because you don't want to fight or due to the lack of knowledge. Don't settle with sowing. We need to gather the harvest. Nobody plants to not harvest. The farmer knows that the reason for his planting is so that in due season, he can gather a good harvest.

SWORDS AND SPEARS

It's time that the church begin to change their farming tools into arms of war. We must not stay with the plowshares and pruninghooks in our hands and go to another level. It's time for us to become warriors in the battlefield; that we would arise and begin to fight for the souls that are held captive by the enemy.

"LET THE WEAK SAY I AM STRONG"

The word "weak" in the original is "chalach" and it means quadriplegic, invalid, paralytic, or someone whose mind is stuck and it's not merely referring to the body, but to the soul and spirit. So then it's not someone who is physically tired, rather someone who is unable to walk spiritually and mentally. Their spirit and mind is in a figurative wheelchair.

This it's the end time church's condition. She's spiritually tired and this is why she no longer wants to fight the battle. The church is in a condition of cerebral palsy. It's time for the church to begin to react and to arise from her wheelchair that she's in. It's time to understand the harvest is ready and there are too few laborers to gather it.

The word "strong" is the word "gibbor" and it means powerful, brave, giant, great, and strong warrior. This verse could read like this: The warriors will arise from their cerebral palsy and be strong and brave warriors. Change your work tools into weapons for war because it's time to gather the harvest.

In order to plant the seed we need farmers but to gather the harvest we need warriors. Not just anyone can gather a harvest. We can be great sowers and bad reapers. That's the condition of the majority of the church. We pass our days planting and planting without a harvest. Vision Crece is precisely for the gathering of the end time harvest. If Jesus said the harvest is already ready, it's because it is. Depends on what type of eyes you are able to see the harvest with.

SOWING WITH GLADNESS

Psalms 126:5-6 *"THEY THAT SOW IN TEARS SHALL REAP IN JOY. HE THAT GOETH FORTH AND WEEPETH, BEARING PRECIOUS SEED, SHALL DOUBTLESS COME AGAIN WITH REJOICING, BRINGING HIS SHEAVES WITH HIM."*

The church has passed its lifetime sowing with tears of pain that are produced by a son or family member not wanting anything with the Lord Jesus Christ. They are tears of sadness when the due to the situation you're living in. The church has shed tears, many tears, and more tears.

But it will not always be so. The time comes when we must rejoice in the harvest. The time comes when we must rejoice, be merry, and happy because the harvest has come. The time of the harvest is now. It's not a happening of tomorrow. No. The time is now. The time must come where you will not be planting and weeping of sadness, rather of happiness and contentment bearing precious seed to plant again.

See what the text is saying. The seed is precious. It's not just any seed.

EVERYTHING THAT IS DONE IN THIS WORLD HAS TO DO WITH SEED

Matthew 13:24 *"ANOTHER PARABLE PUT HE FORTH UNTO THEM, SAYING, THE KINGDOM*

OF HEAVEN IS LIKENED UNTO A MAN WHICH SOWED GOOD SEED IN HIS FIELD:"

Church, everything that is done, be it in word or action, deals with seed. Seed is: your money, words, and actions. Everything is seed. So, the problem is not whether it's seed or not. The problem is the kind of seed you are planting: if your seed is good and precious or evil and ugly. The problem is that humanity has not understood this and it's constantly cursing the seed.

YOUR WORDS ARE YOUR SEED

If you have a close family member who wants nothing with the things of God, might it be that you are cursing your seed? You are always asking God to save your son and to bring him to church, but in your house you are always cursing and using bad language. You are cursing your seed. This is why you aren't harvesting. Your seed is now cursed. We need to understand that everything is seed and that it's precious.

YOUR MONEY IS YOUR SEED

In bringing offerings and tithes, you see money but God sees seed. Now, how are you investing your seed? How are you bringing your seed? Joyfully or angrily? What is your attitude in bringing your offering to the Lord? Or, maybe you aren't even bringing offerings and tithes to the Lord. How, then, do you want to harvest if you're not even planting?

YOUR ACTIONS ARE YOUR SEED

Your actions have to do with your character and your character has to do with who you are. So then, how is your seed in relation to who you are? Are you greedy? Stingy? Or do you plant without fear?

If the Bible says that the seed is precious and good, stop cursing it. Sow with gladness. Once the time comes, you will harvest. What you harvest today is yesterday's planting. What you sow today, you will reap tomorrow. Stop cursing your seed. I cannot imagine a farmer planting and cursing his good and precious seed.

Imagine a farmer. "I curse you." "I hope you don't yield a harvest." "I hope you dry up before anything is born from you." No. Not even the worst farmer would do that. Every farmer sows the seed knowing that one day, he will harvest.

There are two problems the church is going through in relation to the harvest.

FIRST: cursed seed.

SECOND: We don't know how to gather the harvest.

It's what I explained earlier, we have a culture of always speaking negativity and our actions reflect it. But if we speak of the second problem, not knowing how to gather the harvest is causing the loss of souls to the church of the Lord Jesus Christ.

What the church has not understood is that planting and harvesting are not the same. What's the point of planting if in the end I'm not going to harvest? That is a problem that exists in the people of God. We spend our time planting and planting without a harvest.

HARVEST TIME

What's the point of telling people of Christ when I don't know how to care for the harvest? If Jesus said that the harvest is ready, it's because it is. Just like every natural harvest, if the farmer doesn't harvest it in proper time, it will spoil. So, we need to know the exact time to gather this soul harvest. If not, we will lose time in planting again and waiting again for the time until the cycle returns.

It's not that the harvest is not ready; it's that the laborers are not ready to gather the harvest and are ignorant of harvest times. We're losing even our family members. Church, it's necessary to learn to gather the harvest of souls that Christ already has ready for you to gather.

THE HARVEST IS READY

John 4:35 *"DO YOU NOT SAY, 'THERE ARE YET FOUR MONTHS, AND THEN COMES THE HARVEST'? LISTEN! I SAY TO YOU, LIFT UP YOUR EYES AND LOOK AT THE FIELDS, FOR THEY ARE ALREADY WHITE FOR HARVEST."* (MEV)

What Jesus is saying is that every person that comes is a field of wheat. He's not saying that they are sprigs of wheat. They are fields of wheat. What this represents is that if you give the proper importance to each soul that comes and you disciple them well, you cannot know how many more souls they will bring. This is why Jesus spoke to them as fields of wheat and not just sprigs of wheat. Jesus is seeing them with spiritual eyes and not natural ones. The church is just like the disciples, seeing with their natural eyes and waiting four months for the harvest. The church says, "In God's time, my son will come to the feet of Christ." Which is true, but the church has not understood that the time of the Lord is now. That's why He said, "The harvest is now ready."

Church, the time is now: not tomorrow. There are thousands of people being lost daily and the church is doing nothing for them. The problem is not the souls. It's not the harvest. The souls are already ready. The problem here is that there are not enough laborers to gather the harvest.

FEW LABORERS

Matthew 9:37-38 *"THEN SAITH HE UNTO HIS DISCIPLES, THE HARVEST TRULY IS PLENTEOUS, BUT THE LABOURERS ARE FEW; PRAY YE THEREFORE THE LORD OF THE HARVEST, THAT HE WILL SEND FORTH LABOURERS INTO HIS HARVEST."*

Jesus himself said it. The problem is not the harvest; it's ready. The problem is that there aren't capable laborers to gather up that harvest. Jesus did not tell us to pray for the harvest. No. He said we should pray for the laborers, since it's capable laborers that are lacking.

The church has been praying for the souls and not for the laborers. That's why we don't see the results in the harvest. The deal here is that we, pastors, are charged with enabling those laborers so they will gather the harvest. So, where do these laborers come from? From the harvest itself. What's lacking is for time to be dedicated to the harvest you already have in the congregation to prepare them well, and they would then be good laborers to gather the harvest; until it becomes a life cycle.

CONCLUSION

Church, if the farmer of farmers said the harvest is ready, it is. We are lacking the equipped laborers to gather the harvest.

Vision Crece is a vision that comes from the heart of God to prepare laborers to gather the soul harvest that is already ready to receive Jesus as their savior. I recommend that you read this book as many times as necessary until you understand it and if you have any doubts or questions, reach out to us or to someone already applying Vision Crece.

There is a mandate to fulfill and the church doesn't know how. There is no more excuse. This manual will be a great help. Keep on reading and learning. You are about to graduate from Vision Crece. You are in the last chapters of this manual. The following chapters are of vital importance for your life.

Blessings

CHAPTER XI

OPERATIONAL SYSTEM OF VISION CRECE

This chapter is the heart of Vision Crece. So, I expect that you give it the necessary importance and try to learn the operational system of the vision.

John 17:10-12 *"AND ALL MINE ARE THINE, AND THINE ARE MINE; AND I AM GLORIFIED IN THEM. AND NOW I AM NO MORE IN THE WORLD, BUT THESE ARE IN THE WORLD, AND I COME TO THEE. HOLY FATHER, KEEP THROUGH THINE OWN NAME THOSE WHOM THOU HAST GIVEN ME, THAT THEY MAY BE ONE, AS WE ARE. WHILE I WAS WITH THEM IN THE WORLD, I KEPT THEM IN THY NAME: THOSE THAT THOU GAVEST ME I HAVE KEPT, AND NONE OF THEM IS LOST, BUT THE SON OF PERDITION; THAT THE SCRIPTURE MIGHT BE FULFILLED."*

Jesus is referring to the souls in these verses and He is stating that the souls belong to Him. That's the reason He cared for them and not one was lost. Jesus is referring to the care-taking of souls and Vision Crece deals with taking care of souls. The church knows how to win souls for Christ but doesn't know how to care for them.

The operational system of Vision Crece is precisely about the care given souls, but here we will call it consolidation.

OPERATION "3"

Operation 3 is not a new vision or method. None of that. It's simply a tool that will help us to retain the souls within the kingdom of heaven. What the church needs to learn is not how to win souls for Christ since the harvest is already ready. What we need to learn is how to care for the souls. For this reason Jesus said that those He was given, He cared for.

It's pointless for the church to be having event after event and the only ones who attend are the already saved. The truth is that the church has lost the main focus that Jesus had. The kingdom of heaven is about us bringing souls for Christ.

Operation 3 is a tool that serves to restore the design of God for the caring of these souls, just as Jesus did.

NOBODY WANTS TO LOSE THE HARVEST

There is not one pastor, leader, or church member that wants to lose the harvest. But the truth is that we are losing the souls that have already received Jesus as savior. That tells us that things have not been done as Jesus did them. If we want for the harvest that's already been gathered to not be lost within the congregation, it's necessary to make changes in our lives.

Allow me to give you an example. If a builder learned how to build houses incorrectly, his entire life he will build them incorrectly until he recognizes his errors and makes changes.

This is the condition of the modern church. It has good intentions for the souls, but we learned how to do things incorrectly and until we learn to make changes in our life, we won't do things correctly.

HOW DOES OPERATION 3 WORK?

All truth is parallel. What happens in the spiritual happens in the natural and what happens in the natural happens in the spiritual.

THE BIRTH OF A CHILD

Every good doctor knows that when a baby is born the first three days are fundamental for the survival of that baby. In the first three days, without knowing it, that baby has caused a revolution in the hospital. He has one or two nurses that are caring for him and feeding him every three hours. At birth, he was cleansed, bathed, and they placed a bracelet to curb kidnapping on his ankle. There's a doctor in charge of him, a pediatrician, and several specialists in their fields come to check him;

is he breathing normally, is there a defect, and they are in charge to make sure everything is in proper order and at the end of these three days, the doctor in charge will prognoses that everything is okay. You may now take him home. Parting from that moment all the responsibility is now transposed to the mother.

The same thing happens with a person that just accepts Christ as his savior. This person is a newborn baby and needs of all the necessary attentions so that he can survive in his new life.

Operation 3 consists of:
* 3 DAYS
* 3 WEEKS
* 3 TRIMESTERS

That's why it's called Operation 3; because it's based on times of three. If we are able to walk this newborn person to go through this process of times of three, we would be retaining and equipping them to be a great leader who will expand the kingdom of God in the earth.

3 DAYS

The first three days are fundamental to the survival of the newborn. If we are able to consolidate him in those first three days, we will never lose that baby.

THE BEGINNING OF OPERATION 3

- ✓ You make a list of about 3 to 5 people that you want to enter into the kingdom of heaven.
- ✓ They will be interceded for the duration of 40 days in prayer and fasting.
- ✓ You'll pray specifically for their spirit so that it will resurrect or awakened depending on the case.
- ✓ At the end of the last week of those 40 days, physical contact will be made with those on the list.
- ✓ You lead them to either accept Jesus as savior or to a supernatural retreat.

FIRST DAY
- ✓ You speak to him in the morning to see how he's doing. You pray for him and tend to him throughout the day.
- ✓ If they've accepted Jesus as savior then we will gift them a small book called, "My Connection With God" which has daily declarations that the baby should repeat.
- ✓ If he is already saved then we speak to them about the process of restoration they should live.
- ✓ Parting from that moment you should never leave that baby alone. A war has just begun for the soul of that baby.

- ✓ On the first day you visit them at their home and if necessary and the opportunity presents itself you make a declaration of peace.
- ✓ Beginning on that first day he is fed 3 times a day, morning, noon, and night by phone, text, message, visit, or a coffee meet.
- ✓ From the very first day, you become his shadow.
- ✓ You are for him, his nurse, doctor, specialist, and the spiritual father of that baby.
- ✓ You clean him, care for him, feed him, and tend to him, spiritually speaking.
- ✓ Remember, the enemy is fighting for him and if you leave him alone for a moment, he will snatch him out of your hands.
- ✓ Jesus has already done a work in him. Now it's up to you to care for him the way He did with the souls. And, if the enemy snatches him out of my hands, He will call me into account one day.

SECOND DAY
- ✓ You call him in the morning and see how he's doing and you pray for him.
- ✓ You should visit or meet with him somewhere. Do not leave him alone.
- ✓ You call in the afternoon and evening to check on him and pray for him.
- ✓ Don't allow anyone or anything to snatch him out of your hands.
- ✓ Remember that there are thousands of demons using his relatives and friends to take him out of the kingdom of heaven.

- ✓ You begin to tell him about the processes of restoration.
- ✓ Remind him of the daily declarations from the booklet.

THIRD DAY

- ✓ You speak to him in the morning. You greet him and pray for him. You cover him with the blood of Jesus.
- ✓ You share with him the type of ministry we are. What we believe and preach.
- ✓ Remember that he is a baby and that it has only been three days since birth.
- ✓ Don't leave him alone. Care for him. He's your son. He needs you.
- ✓ You are his shadow. Visit him. Take him out for fun.
- ✓ This third day is fundamental.
- ✓ Jesus resurrected on the third day. Paul recovered sight on the third day. The third day is a day of resurrection. It's a day when the scales fall from our eyes.
- ✓ If you were able to help this baby stay alive spiritually on this day, you accomplished the first part of Operation 3.
- ✓ At nighttime you dismiss with a word of prayer.

THE FOUR FOLLOWING WEEKS AFTER THAT WEEK

DAY FOUR AND FIVE
- ✓ Continue making contact with him, just like on the first three days.
- ✓ We'll be making use of different materials from the church: the church's channel, testimonies from church, etc. You'll download some Christian music for him. Who we are as a church, etc.
- ✓ You visit again on the fifth day.
- ✓ At night, pray for him and dismiss yourself.

DAYS SIX AND SEVEN
- ✓ Continue doing the same. Don't leave him alone, praying for and feeding him.
- ✓ Remember that he has the booklet called "My Connection With God."
- ✓ It contains declarations for the seven days.
- ✓ On the seventh day you will give him another book titled "School of D.B.H." (Deliverance, Blessing, and Healing)

D.B.H. SCHOOL
- ✓ It's a book that contains 21 lessons: one per day.
- ✓ 7 about Deliverance, 7 about Blessing, and 7 of Healing.
- ✓ You give him the task of reading it at home and twice a week you gather in order to minister to him.

✓ Every day over the phone you can handle any questions they might have about the lessons.

✓ When he is finished with the D.B.H. school, a month has passed.

✓ It's been a month where you did not leave them alone for a moment.

✓ At the end of this month of consolidation we will plan a party of welcome and give him a diploma from the D.B.H. school.

✓ After finishing with the D.B.H. school, he will then be invited to a three day supernatural retreat.

SUPERNATURAL RETREAT

✓ Bring that baby who was born about a month ago to church to a three day supernatural retreat.

✓ During that weekend we minister healing of the soul to him.

✓ We minister deliverance to different areas of his life.

✓ We begin on a Friday evening and end Sunday evening.

✓ By that Sunday, he is a completely changed person.

✓ We speak to him about baptism.

✓ We invite him to the scheduled services at church and encourage them to continue forward without abandoning them.

✓ Remember that he has no one but you. You are his spiritual father.

DELIVERANCE

- ✓ Once that person has lived a retreat he is then invited to go through deliverance.
- ✓ This would be a personalized deliverance and it's done however many times it's necessary.
- ✓ He's invited to purchase (or one is given to him) a book called "Manual Of Deliverance" so they can begin to learn what the ministry of deliverance is.
- ✓ You recommend he buys the book titled "7 Keys to Deliverance."
- ✓ He has to see them within two months…and we minister deliverance through each one.
- ✓ One week after he is done with the '"Seven Keys to Deliverance," he then goes on to the school of discipleship.

THREE TRIMESTERS

- ✓ Recommend that he buy the three discipleship books.
- ✓ It's nine months of discipleship material.
- ✓ One every three months.
- ✓ First trimester: Restoring Your Identity.
- ✓ Second trimester: The Message of the Kingdom.
- ✓ Third trimester: Spiritual Warfare
- ✓ By this time the disciple has matured.
- ✓ The next and final step is to send him.

SEND

The final step of "sending" is the last in the process of Vision Crece, since by this time a year has passed in which he has learned all about the vision. He is now ready to apply Vision Crece.

To "send" is that this soul who is no longer a baby can now do the same with someone else.

CONCLUSION

I expect that this manual of soul retention can be a great help and you apply it to the babies that God gives you. If you have any doubts or questions, make the effort to contact me to the number at the beginning of this book.

Blessings

CHAPTER XII

CASTING THE NET

This is the last chapter of Vision Crece. It's time to put into practice everything learned in Vision Crece.

Casting the net is to begin to gather the readied harvest: it's speaking to the souls about what Jesus did for them, it's to liberate the captive, it's to heal the sick, it's to lift the fallen, it's rescuing the lost, it's comforting the needy, it's to heal the brokenhearted, it's preaching the kingdom, its loving your neighbor, it's having compassion for souls, it's casting out demons, it's souls recovering their identity, it's for souls to return to their original created state, it's restoring them, it's coming out of your comfort zone, it's sacrificing, it's investing time, money, and effort, it's giving it all for a soul, and finally, casting the net is to be sent as Jesus was sent.

Luke 5:1-11 *"AND IT CAME TO PASS, THAT, AS THE PEOPLE PRESSED UPON HIM TO HEAR THE WORD OF GOD, HE STOOD BY THE LAKE OF GENNESARET, AND SAW TWO SHIPS STANDING BY THE LAKE: BUT THE FISHERMEN WERE GONE OUT OF THEM, AND WERE WASHING THEIR NETS. AND HE ENTERED INTO ONE OF THE SHIPS, WHICH WAS SIMON'S, AND PRAYED THAT HE WOULD*

THRUST OUT A LITTLE FROM THE LAND. AND HE SAT DOWN, AND TAUGHT THE PEOPLE OUT OF THE SHIP. NOW WHEN HE HAD LEFT SPEAKING, HE SAID UNTO SIMON, LAUNCH OUT INTO THE DEEP, AND LET DOWN YOUR NETS FOR A DRAUGHT. AND SIMON ANSWERING SAID UNTO HIM, MASTER, WE HAVE TOILED ALL THE NIGHT, AND HAVE TAKEN NOTHING: NEVERTHELESS AT THY WORD I WILL LET DOWN THE NET. AND WHEN THEY HAD THIS DONE, THEY INCLOSED A GREAT MULTITUDE OF FISHES: AND THEIR NET BROKE. AND THEY BECKONED UNTO THEIR PARTNERS, WHICH WERE IN THE OTHER SHIP, THAT THEY SHOULD COME AND HELP THEM. AND THEY CAME, AND FILLED BOTH THE SHIPS, SO THAT THEY BEGAN TO SINK. WHEN SIMON PETER SAW IT, HE FELL DOWN AT JESUS' KNEES, SAYING, DEPART FROM ME; FOR I AM A SINFUL MAN, O LORD. FOR HE WAS ASTONISHED, AND ALL THAT WERE WITH HIM, AT THE DRAUGHT OF THE FISHES WHICH HAD BEN TAKEN: AND SO WAS ALSO JAMES, AND JOHN, THE SONS OF ZEBEDEE, WHICH WERE PARTNERS WITH SIMON. AND JESUS SAID UNTO SIMON, FEAR NOT; FROM HENCEFORTH THOU SHALT CATCH MEN. AND WHEN THEY HAD BROUGHT THEIR SHIPS TO LAND, THEY FORSOOK ALL, AND FOLLOWED HIM."

In this passage that we just saw, it tells us about the miraculous catch and it's true. To rescue the lost is a true miracle. I just want to bring to the forefront a couple of key texts in this scripture. In verse 2 it tells us that two boats were on the shore. If we want to gather a harvest of souls in the last days, we need to get away from the shore. The church needs to get away from just hanging around the shore. To be at the shore is to be satisfied with just about anything. We are satisfied with the small things when God has great things for us. Hanging around the shore is to be satisfied with two or three souls for Christ. Hanging around the shore is to be happy with raising a church, when we can raise many more. Being at the shore represents that we are not satisfied with gaining one city for the kingdom when we can gain many cities for Christ.

We need to stop navigating the shores and thrust into the deep. In verse 4 Jesus gives the word to Simon to thrust away from land. Only away from land can you find the great catch. The fish are not found by the beach; rather they are in the depths of the sea. If we want to catch the greatest catch of souls we have ever seen, we need to learn to thrust into the deep.

Thrusting into the deep represents:
- More intimacy with God.
- That I am no longer satisfied with what God has already given me, instead I want more every day.
- To no longer just be in the shallow parts.
- Wanting more of Him.

- Gathering the already ready harvest.
- My duty to expand the kingdom of heaven here on the earth.
- Stop playing the Christian game and begin to do the will of God.

In verse 5 Simon responds to Jesus saying that he's been working all night without catching anything, but he would do it at His Word. Simon and his partners were tired from casting the net many times without any catch.

That's how we find the church today; tired of casting the net without a catch to show for it. That's how nights, months, and years pass, fruitless. It's because we've spent our time at the seashore. What God wants is for us to not be satisfied with what He has already given us, but we need to thrust out into the deep and cast the net at His Word. That's why the church is getting tired, because she's done everything in her power but not in His Word. Let's cast the net in His Name and we will see the harvest of souls like we've never seen before.

Casting the net in His Word and in the depths of the sea is to trust and depend on Him. This is what is lacking in the church of the Lord Jesus Christ: to know how to depend on Him. The church in these last centuries has done things how she wants them done and not how He wants them done.

CONCLUSION

Church, it's necessary for us to understand that there are a multitude of souls that are perishing daily and it's our responsibility to speak to them of Christ. It's time to cast the net and begin to catch the greatest number of fish in the depths of the sea.

This book is very useful to help you start harvesting. Apply Vision Crece in your life and ministry and you'll see the harvest as your eyes have never seen. I expect Vision Crece to be a great blessing and soon you'll see the fruit of it in your life.

Any questions you might have about Vision Crece, call 325.603.6230 or send us an email: info@e220.church

Blessings

E220 CHURCH

Write to:

E220 Church
1241 Cypress St
Abilene, TX 79601

Telephone: 325.603.6230

Email: info@e220.church

Webpage: www.e220.church

facebook.com/E220church